# · Bartholomew ·

# *WALK SKYE & WESTER ROSS*

## *Richard Hallewell*

Bartholomew

*A Division of* HarperCollins*Publishers*

Published by Bartholomew
HarperCollins*Publishers*
77-85 Fulham Palace Road
London W6 8JB


A catalogue record for this book
is available from the British Library.


First published 1993
© Bartholomew 1993


Printed in Great Britain by Bartholomew,
The Edinburgh Press Limited.
Typesetting by John McKinlay, 11 King Street, Perth.

ISBN 0-7028-2176-0

93/1/16 BNM

Britain's landscape is changing all the time. While every
care has been taken in the preparation of this guide,
Bartholomew accepts no responsibility whatsoever for any
loss, damage, injury or inconvenience sustained or caused as
a result of using this guide.

# CONTENTS

| Walk | Grade | | | | Walk | Grade | | | |
|---|---|---|---|---|---|---|---|---|---|
| 1 Stac Pollaidh | B | 🥾 | | | 18 Munlochy Bay | B/C | wc | | 🚌 |
| 2 Rhue Lighthouse | B | wc | | 🚌 | 19 Quiraing | A | 🥾 | | |
| 3 Loch Achall | B | wc | 🥾 | 🚌 | 20 Old Man of Storr | B | 🥾 | | 🚌 |
| 4 Mellon Udrigle | B | | | | 21 Portree Loop | B | wc | | 🚌 |
| 5 Poolewe to Fionn Loch | A/B/C | | | | 22 Waternish Point | A | | | |
| 6 Flowerdale Forest | B/C | wc | | 🚌 | 23 Waternish Loop | B | | | 🚌 |
| 7 Red Point to Diabaig | A | 🥾 | | 🚌 | 24 Coral Beaches | C | | | 🚌 |
| 8 Beinn Eighe | A/C | 🥾 | | 🚌 | 25 Neist Point | C | | | |
| 9 Coire Mhic Fhearchair | A | 🥾 | | 🚌 | 26 Oronsay | C | | | |
| 10 Leacanashie | B | | | | 27 Talisker | B | 🥾 | | 🚌 |
| 11 Plockton Loop | B/C | wc | 🐕 | 🚌 | 28 Glenbrittle | A | wc | 🥾 | |
| 12 Balmacara Forest Walk | B | 🐕 | | | 29 Elgol | A/B | wc | 🥾 | 🚌 |
| 13 Falls of Glomach | A | 🥾 | | | 30 Point of Sleat | B | | | |
| 14 Fyrish Monument | B | 🐕 | | | 31 Hallaig | A/B | 🥾 | | 🚌 |
| 15 Knock Farrel | B/C | wc | 🐕 | | 32 Loch Oich | B | | | |
| 16 Chanonry Point | C | wc | | 🚌 | 33 Caig Forest Walk | C | | 🐕 | |
| 17 Fortrose to Avoch | B | wc | | 🚌 | 34 Ben Nevis | A | wc | 🥾 | 🚌 |
| | | | | | 35 Achriabhach Forest Walk | C | | 🐕 | 🚌 |

## Symbols

**wc**    Public conveniences available at route, or in nearby town. (NB: these facilities are often closed in the winter.)

    Hill walking equipment required: strong boots and waterproof clothing. Detailed map and compass recommended.

    Route suitable for dogs.

    Public transport available to this route. Details given on individual routes.

## Grades

**A**    Difficult route. Requires a high level of fitness and some previous experience of hill walking. The use of a detailed area map is advised.

**B**    Moderate route, suitable for most people. Requires a reasonabe level of fitness. Book map sufficient.

**C**    A simple, easy walk on good paths.

# *About this book*

This guide contains a selection of walks in the Isle of Skye, Wester and Easter Ross, the Black Isle and Lochaber. All of these routes follow generally accepted footpaths and Rights of Way and can easily be completed within one day. They are scattered throughout this large area, and visit many of its famous places and areas of most dramatic mountain and coastal scenery.

Each route is graded according to its level of difficulty, and wherever specialist hill-walking equipment is required this is specified on the contents page. There is a description of each route, including information on the character and condition of the paths, and a brief description of the major points of interest along the way, plus a detailed sketch map of the route to aid navigation. This guide supplies all the necessary information to complete each walk as long as the weather and visibility are good. In bad weather and low visibility, however, the use of a detailed map and compass are strongly advised on all hill routes, while it is suggested that these be carried on all Grade A routes as a matter of course.

Car parks, where available, are indicated on the route maps; in many cases, however, it is necessary to park by the roadside. When this is the case, please take all care to avoid blocking the road, passing places (on single-track roads) or field entrances. The availability of public conveniences and public transport on particular routes is listed on the contents page and at the start of each walk. The location of all the routes is shown on the area map at the front of the book. At the beginning of the write-up of each walk there is a brief description of how the start of the route can be reached by car from the largest nearby town.

The following introduction provides a summary of the geography, history and wildlife of the area, plus a short guide to some of the more common elements in the Gaelic place names of the area. There is also a section of advice to walkers which you should read before setting out.

## Key

| | | |
|---|---|---|
| •••• Route | ••❭• Direction of route | **1 foot = 0.3m** |
| ═══ Metalled Road | wc Public convenience | **1 mile = 1.6km** |
| ++++ Railway | ♠♠ Coniferous woodland | |
| Ⓟ Parking | ♦♦ Broad-leaved woodland | |
| Contour: shaded area is above height indicated | *i* Tourist information centre | |

## The Area

*(Figures in italics refer to individual walks)*

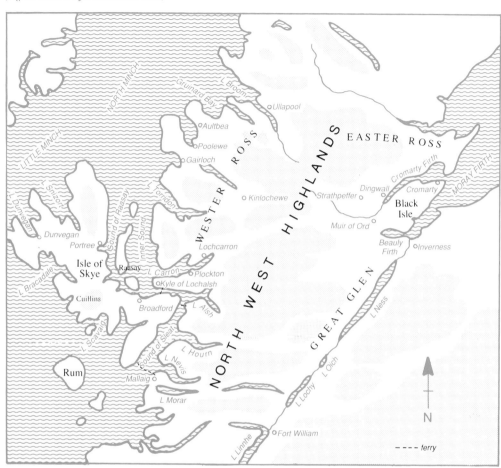

This is a large area – over 100 miles (160km) from Neist Point *(25)* on the western coast of Skye to Sutor Stacks at the tip of the Black Isle, and almost as far from the scree slopes of Stac Pollaidh *(1)* in the north to Glen Nevis *(34,35)* in the south. Within this area lies some of the finest walking in the British Isles, ranging from the rugged hill paths of Skye and Wester Ross to the gentler routes of the peninsulas of the Black Isle and Easter Ross. No selection can hope to do complete justice to such a choice, but this guide should provide a suitable introduction to the available pleasures and an indication of what types of walking can be encountered where. Those who develop a taste for the area will find plenty more routes in all quarters.

In political terms, this area falls completely within the boundaries of the huge Highland Region, governed from its headquarters in Inverness. More meaningfully, perhaps, it encompasses the greater part of the the old county of Ross and Cromarty plus the western part of Invernesshire. The broad wedge of the area is widest in the west, where a ragged fringe of sea lochs, headlands and islands, abuts the Atlantic Ocean. Most of the land in the west is over 600ft/183m above sea-level and much is above 1400ft/427m. Like most of northern

Scotland it is on the very edge of the area of comfortable human habitation: the population is small, and settlements are scattered thinly on the low land by the coast and along the occasional fertile glen.

When the last Ice Age retreated, some 8000 years ago, a landscape was revealed of steep-sided hills separated by wide valleys. The hills had been scraped down to the rock by the action of the glaciers: cracked and torn into dramatic peaks and narrow, broken ridges. The valleys were gouged into broad, U-shaped profiles, and were filled, in places, by saltwater inlets and freshwater lochs. The land was a poor, infertile one, but the landscape was, and remains, heroic in scale and form.

The most northerly section of coast covered is that of **Wester Ross**; running from the northern boundary south to Loch Alsh and the kyles (narrows) between Skye and the mainland. The major sea lochs (running north to south) are Loch Broom *(2,3)*, Little Loch Broom, Gruinard Bay *(4)*, Loch Ewe *(5)*, Loch Gairloch *(6)*, Loch Torridon *(7)*, Loch Kishorn and Loch Carron *(10)*. The only sizable inland lochs are Fionn Loch *(5)* and the splendid Loch Maree *(8)* – 12 miles (19km) long and 2 miles (3km) wide at its widest; scattered with wooded islands and surrounded by some of the finest scenery in the region.

There are only three towns of any size on this stretch of coast: the 18th-century fishing harbour (now the terminus for the Stornoway ferry) of Ullapool *(2,3)* in the north and Lochcarron and Kyle of Lochalsh in the south. In a country where the charm of the towns is rarely a match for that of the scenery, Ullapool, with its rows of whitewashed buildings arranged on a low spit of land jutting into Loch Broom, is a pleasant exception. These apart, there are only a few scattered villages: Aultbea, Poolewe *(5)*, Gairloch, Shieldaig and the charming resort of Plockton *(11)* along the coast, with Kinlochewe at the head of Loch Maree. Of these, Gairloch (with neighbouring Charlestown) *(6)* is the largest.

Wester Ross has long been a favourite destination for walkers. In particular, the line of sandstone hills running south from Stac Pollaidh, and including An Teallach (south of Little Loch

Broom) and the group of Munros around the head of Loch Torridon *(9)*, has proved a great attraction. The coast also has a peculiar charm, with its mixture of rocky headlands and fine sand beaches backed by dunes and calcium-rich grassland *(4,7)*. The band containing the finest scenery is quite narrow, however: once off the sandstone and out of sight of the deep inlets of the Atlantic, the hills lose their distinctive silhouettes and colouring and the landscape grows bleaker.

The landscape of the **Isle of Skye** is just as exciting as that of Wester Ross, but geologically the two areas are very different. Skye (apart from the Torridonian sandstone and gneiss of the southern part of the island) is composed of igneous rocks: basalt, granite and gabbro, formed when the molten magma from the interior of the Earth emerged onto the surface and cooled. These are hard rocks, which have produced, in places, some very dramatic effects: notably in the ridge of Trotternish *(19,20)* and the Cuillin Hills.

The island measures some 50 miles (80km) from Rubha Hunish in the north to the Point of Sleat *(30)* in the south, and around 25 miles (40km) at its widest point, between Neist Point *(25)* in the west and the eastern coast of Trotternish. The coastline is greatly indented, however, and the total land area is only around 670 square miles. The island is generally mountainous, but the peaks are low outside the tight group which constitutes the Cuillins: a tangled mass of rocky summits, ridges and corries, whose skyline is one of the finest sights in the Highlands. None of the routes in this guide enters the range (some experience of climbing is needed before venturing onto the steep slopes), but two of them *(28,29)* pass close by and provide fine views.

The narrows between Skye and mainland – the Inner Sound in the north and the Sound of Sleat in the south – are crossed by three ferry services: Kyle of Lochalsh to Kyleakin being the main one, with the other two crossing at Kylerhea-Glenelg and Armadale-Mallaig (a bridge is currently proposed for the Kyleakin crossing). The main sea lochs around the island are Loch Snizort and Loch Dunvegan *(24)* in the north, and Lochs Bracadale *(26)*, Scavaig *(29)* and Slapin in the west. The only large freshwater loch is Loch Coruisk, in the Cuillins, but there are numerous small rivers which are famous for their salmon and trout.

What little arable land there is is largely confined to the small-scale crofts along the coastal strip. The rest of the island is given over to rough sheep and cattle grazing, moorland and some forestry. The small population is scattered thinly around the coast of the island, sometimes collected into small crofting townships, but only forming towns at the island capital of Portree *(21)*, and (to a lesser degree) at Dunvegan *(24)*, Broadford and Kyleakin.

There are numerous smaller islands off the coast of Skye. The largest of these is Raasay *(31)*, in the Inner Sound, which can only be reached by ferry from Skye. Amongst the many smaller, uninhabited, islands is Oronsay *(26)* in Loch Bracadale, which can be reached on foot at low tide.

Back on the mainland, the coast south of Loch Alsh and Loch Duich is even less populous than that of Wester Ross, and large areas of it are virtually inaccessible. Beyond the head of Loch Duich are the steep, grassy slopes of the Five Sisters of Kintail – a line of peaks reaching over 3000ft (910m) – and to the west of those is a hilly peninsula along which a narrow road leads to the village of Glenelg and the Kylerhea ferry for Skye. To the south of this peninsula is Loch Hourn, and beyond that is Knoydart: a truly wild area, accessible only on foot or by the small passenger ferry from Mallaig.

Inland from west coast of the area, around the watershed of the North West Highlands, is an area of heather hills and moorland, cut by a number of large glens and crossed by a few roads, but largely unpopulated. It is an area with its own charm (particularly in the glens carrying the upper waters of the River Beauly: Glens Strathfarrar, Cannich and Affric), but as its best routes are either over-long or inaccessible they are not covered in this guide.

To the east of this, at the narrow point of the wedge, is the only region of large-scale arable farming in this area: the **Black Isle** *(16,17,18)* – not actually an island, but almost cut off by the long inlets of the Cromarty Firth and the Beauly Firth. The highest part of the peninsula is given over to forestry and some moorland, but otherwise this is an area of farmland, criss-crossed by numerous roads. The walks here are generally short and gentle.

The main towns on the Black Isle are Cromarty (a fine old town, worth a visit on its own account), Rosemarkie and Fortrose *(16,17)*. At the head of the Cromarty Firth is the larger town of Dingwall, with the old spa resort of Strathpeffer *(15)* in the low hills beyond, and Conon Bridge, Muir of Ord and Beauly in the low-lying neck of land between the heads of the two firths. Across the Kessock Bridge from the Black Isle is the large town of Inverness: the main service centre for the northern Highlands.

The eastern edge of the Black Isle runs – Chanonry Ness apart *(16)* – as straight as a slide rule; following the line of a major fault line. Beyond Inverness, this fault line continues as the **Great Glen**; a steep-sided valley running approximately 60 miles (95km) south-west to Fort William at the head of Loch Linnhe. The Caledonian Canal (1804-47) follows the line of the Glen, running 22 miles (35km) as a true canal, and for the other 38 miles (60km) making use of Lochs Ness, Oich *(32)* and Lochy (naming them from north to south).

Fort William is a large town and a good centre: apart from the road north to Inverness, the town sits at the crossroads of routes to Mallaig (and thence to Skye by the ferry), Speyside and, to the south, Oban and Argyll. There is fine hill-walking in the area, particularly on Ben Nevis *(34)* and amongst the peaks to the east and south, while the West Highland Way (long-distance footpath) heads southwards from the town through Glen Coe and Rannoch Moor to Loch Lomond.

# History

The visitor who arrives in the north of Scotland ignorant of the region's history will find little to enlighten him. Outside the eastern end of the area there are few obvious memorials: castles, churches, monuments and towns. The Gaels of the west built little that was meant to last.

Nevertheless, Highland history is a particularly interesting subject, since the society which developed in the area was signally different from anything else which evolved on the British mainland, and it survived, almost unchanged, from the Dark Ages well into the modern period.

The earliest known inhabitants of the area were the Picts, whose various tribes occupied all of northern Scotland. They posed a serious threat to the northern boundaries of Roman occupation in Britain, yet their culture and language were subsequently to disappear almost entirely. They may have been of Celtic origin, but it is impossible to know for certain, and the only relics which they left were some items of metalwork, a collection of impressive stone carvings of uncertain purpose, and the advanced defensive structures known as brochs.

The carvings are thought to have been produced between the sixth and the tenth centuries. The earlier examples are decorated with abstract symbols and schematic animal forms, and may have represented family or tribal relationships; the later stones carry religious motifs. Most of the stones discovered in Scotland have been found to the south of this area, but a few have come to light in the Black Isle, and two in Skye.

The distribution of the brochs (the products of an earlier perioid: around the start of the first century) is somewhat different: virtually all the substantial examples are situated in the north of the country and in the northern and western islands. The broch was a circular dry-stone tower, probably varying from 15 to 50 feet (4.6-15.2m) in height and with a single entrance. It was a defensive structure of the crudest form (presumably used as a refuge for surrounding tribesmen), yet the skill shown in the construction is often considerable.

The best examples in this area are Dun Telve and Dun Troddan, within a short distance of each other east of Glenelg (near the mainland end of the Kylerhea ferry to Skye), which are now retained in a well-preserved condition. Two less complete examples can be found near the path to Waternish Point on Skye *(22)*.

From the 6th century onwards the Pictish communities throughout Scotland were increasingly on the defensive; harried in the south by the Britons and the Angles, and in the west by the Scots: a Celtic warrior-aristocracy which arrived from Ireland around 500 and established itself in the small kingdom of Dalriada in Argyll. The Scots were Gaelic-speaking and Christian, and their language and culture would gradually colonise virtually all of the area of modern Scotland.

In part, this was made possible by a further threat to all the tribes of Scotland: the increasing raids on the north and west, from around 800 onwards, by the Vikings. These coastal attacks affected both the Scots and the Picts, who seem to have moved inland under the pressure and may have been forced to work in concert to defend their territories. In 843 this trend was taken to its logical conclusion and the two kingdoms were unified under the Scot, Kenneth McAlpin.

The Vikings, meanwhile, established themselves in the northern and western islands, and (to a lesser extent) on the adjacent mainland. In succeeding generations they mingled with the existing populations of Picts and Scots to produce the mixed race of the Gallgaels ('foreigner-Gaels'). The resulting cultural mix varied from area to area: in the Northern and Western Isles the population largely adopted Norse language and customs, but elsewhere the earlier cultures survived in parallel (this seems to have occurred in Skye). Nevertheless, the Hebrides remained under the overlordship of the Norwegian crown until after Alexander III had defeated King Haakon of Norway at the Battle of Largs (1263). Following this, Gaelic language and culture gradually ousted the Norse influence, until it had completely disappeared from the Highlands and western islands.

The net result of these various invasions was to create a society with strong warlike traditions and a disinclination to accept the nominal central control of the Scottish monarchy; a control which the monarchy – Norman and increasingly anglicised – could never fully enforce. As a result, a distinctive social organisation developed north of the Highland Line – tribal and semi-anarchic – which would survive until the greater powers of the Crown and Parliament of Great Britain could be turned against it in the 18th century.

The clan system emerged around the 13th century. It was based upon the unit of the family group – 'clann' means 'children' – and although it became flexible to the extent that individuals, or indeed whole clans, could ally themselves to a local power irrespective of any family relationship, the notion of kinship remained a part of the idea of the clan, and made the relationship between the chief and his clansmen different from the more strictly legal ties binding (for example) a feudal overlord and his vassal.

Warfare was part of the culture of the Highlanders, and although it would be inaccurate to suggest that the clansmen were perpetually at war with each other, it is true that feuding was endemic, and that individual inter-clan wars could be of very long duration. No single power ever evolved in the Highlands which was sufficiently strong to enforce a lasting peace, so disputes could only be ended by either the complete victory of one of the antagonists or the intervention of neighbouring clans.

The nearest thing to a central government of Gaelic Scotland was the Lordship of the Isles: a hereditary title held by the MacDonalds. It was based upon the memory of Norse independence in the islands, but at its height extending to include much of the Gaelic-speaking mainland. A plot entered into by John of the Isles (whereby the Lordship would become an independent kingdom beneath the overlordship of the English king) led ultimately to the forfeiture of the title to the Scottish Crown in 1493. Thereafter, the Highlands lacked any single power strong enough to ensure internal stability.

There were a number of branches of the powerful Clan Donald within this area: the MacDonalds of Sleat *(30)*, in the south of Skye (the Clan Donald museum is at Armadale), and also in the north of the island in Trotternish *(19,20)* (from where they expelled the MacLeods); the MacDonells of Glengarry, with their main stronghold at Invergarry on Loch Oich *(32)*; and the MacDonalds of Clanranald in the south-west. In addition to these, the main clans in the region were the MacLeods in the west of Skye (where Dunvegan remains the seat of the chief) *(24)* and in

Raasay *(31)*, and the Mackinnons in the east of the island. The lower end of the Great Glen was held by the Camerons, while the land to the west of Loch Ness was in the hands of the Grants, with the Chisholms in Glen Affric to the west of that. At the northern end of the Great Glen were the Frasers. The Urquharts owned land in the Black Isle until the 17th century, while the Munros inhabited the land to the north of the Cromarty Firth. Apart from these, most of the land in this area ultimately fell into the hands of the powerful MacKenzies, who pursued a policy of supporting the forces of central authority against their neighbours and prospered mightily as a result. The burial place of the MacKenzies of Seaforth is in Fortrose Cathedral *(16)*; a short walk from Chanonry Point. This is traditionally believed to be the place of execution of the Brahan seer: the famous soothsayer who is said to have forecast the extinction of the line of Seaforth.

There are few accessible architectural remains of the clan period in the area which are not ruined. Apart from Dunvegan, the most impressive is the much-photographed Eilean Donan Castle on its island in Loch Duich (east of Kyle of Lochalsh on the A87), of which the MacRaes were hereditary constables for the MacKenzies. The castle was largely destroyed in the 18th century, but was rebuilt in the 1930s and is now open to the public.

Following the defeat of the Jacobites at Culloden, in 1746, clan society and the culture which it fostered began to disintegrate. The chiefs became landlords rather than the fathers of their tribe, and discovered a more pressing need for funds than for armed clansmen – particularly as these could no longer bear arms. Those who wished to continue the tradition of following a fighting life joined the newly formed Highland regiments and fought abroad for the Hanoverian monarchy; those who didn't left for the factories in the south or emigrated to the New World, either willingly or otherwise. In the Highlands, the inland glens were largely cleared for sheep farming, and the population was moved down to the coast. Some attempt was made to provide alternative employment by establishing a herring industry along the coast, but although the British Fisheries

Society founded the village and harbour at Ullapool *(2,3)* in 1788, it was the east coast of Caithness and Sutherland which prospered most from the burgeoning industry.

Apart from Fort William *(34)*, this area has largely missed out on large-scale industrial development. However, there is one relic of the early Industrial Revolution which is worthy of note: the Caledonian Canal. This was surveyed by Thomas Telford in 1804, but was not finally completed until 1847.

# Place Names

Most of the place names in the area covered by this guide are Gaelic: a language now known to comparatively few (though you will probably hear it spoken on Skye). As a knowledge of the more common elements can add to the pleasure of walking in the area, and can also be of some help in map reading, I have included a short list below. Even now, a certain amount of guesswork will be required, as the words which appear on the map will, as often as not, be slightly different from those shown here. In the eastern part of the area (where Gaelic has not been generally spoken for some time) and near the busier thoroughfares, words will often have been anglicised – eg: *Knock* for *Cnoc (15)*. In the more isolated areas of the west, where the language is still spoken, the names will be more grammatically correct, and will thus be altered by aspiration, the addition of letters to denote case, etc.

Gaelic is not the only language to have been spoken in this area, and place names can suggest the extent of the influence of the various peoples who have inhabited this part of Scotland through the centuries. Having said that, there are limitations to the effectiveness of this system: the Picts – who once inhabited all of this area; though not, presumably, in large numbers – have left virtually no indication of their presence in this form.

The vikings were rather more influential, and a number of quite common Norse elements can be found; particularly in Skye and on the western seaboard. *Dale* for valley, *-ay* for an island (Raasay, Oronsay), *-val* for a hill (Stockval, Healabhal: both in Skye), *-nish* for a headland (Trotternish, Ullnish, etc). These can sometimes be found with added Gaelic elements (Healabhal Mhor), while occasionally the Norse word has simply been adopted by the Gaelic language (*Sgeir* from the Norse *Sker*).

## Common Elements in Place Names: Gaelic unless otherwise stated

| | | |
|---|---|---|
| Aber - *Confluence* | Carn/Cairn - *Hill, heap of stones* | Leitir - *Extensive slope* |
| Abhainn - *River* | Cnoc/Knock - *Hillock* | Lochan - *Small loch* |
| Acarsaid - *Harbour* | Coire - *Corrie (hollow)* | Meall - *Rounded hill* |
| Ach/Achadh - *Field* | Creag, Craig - *Rock, cliff* | Mor - *Big* |
| Allt - *Burn* | Dale/Dal - *Valley (Norse)* | Ruadh - *Red* |
| Aird - *Promontory* | Dubh - *Black* | Rubha - *Point of land* |
| -ay/-ey - *Island (Norse)* | Dun - *Steep hill, fort* | Sgeir/Skerry - *Rock surrounded by sea* |
| Bal/Baile - *Town, settlement* | Eilean - *Island* | Sgurr - *Peak, sharp top* |
| Beag/Beg - *Small* | Firth - *Arm of the sea (Norse)* | Sron - *Nose, point* |
| Bealach - *Hill pass* | Glas - *Grey* | Stac - *Rocky column, cliff* |
| Beinn/Ben - *Mountain* | Inver - *River mouth* | Storr - *Steep, high peak* |
| Breac - *Speckled* | Kil - *Church* | Tobar - *Well* |
| Buidhe - *Yellow* | Kyle/Caol - *Narrow strait* | -val - *Mountain (Norse)* |
| Camas - *Bay* | Leacann - *Slope* | |

# Natural History

In an area so large, there is naturally a wide variety of habitats: from the high tops and moorland of the west to the farmland and mud-flats of the Black Isle. In order to describe the wildlife of the region, it is useful to provide a number of broad headings for the various habitats – **Mountains and Moorland, Seashore, Freshwater, Conifer Woodland, Broad-leaved Woodland, Farmland** – and then to note the particular birds and animals which the walker may expect to see in each. This has been done below, and the routes which particularly feature each habitat are listed beside the relevant heading. Naturally, it is impossible to be entirely accurate with such a brief study, and great good fortune is required to see some of the rare or nocturnal species, but this should give a rough indication of the wildlife which might be seen along the way.

## Mountains and Moorland *(1,3,5,6,7,8,9,11,14,19, 20,22,23,27,28,29,30,31,34)*

The vast majority of the area falls under this heading. With the poor soils and heavy rainfall in the western part of the Highlands, moorland – generally confined to the higher slopes in the east – often remains the prevalent land cover right down to sea-level. In the centre and eastern part of the area, the cover is generally **ling** and **bell heather**, but in the west this often gives way to a rocky grassland.

The higher slopes *(8,34)* are rocky and virtually bare. The generally low temperatures and high winds maintain sub-alpine conditions, with pockets of snow lasting well into the summer on northern slopes. Some **ptarmigan**, the hardiest of the grouse family, may be seen near the tops, or lower in winter, but little else.

On the lower moors **red grouse** are present, with some **black grouse** (generally on the margins of woodland) in the east and south. The **wheatear** is common throughout the area during the summer, while the **stonechat** is present throughout the year. Of the waders, **snipe, curlew, golden plover, redshank** and **greenshank** are present, as are three types of falcon – **peregrine, kestrel** and **merlin** – plus the **buzzard, hen harrier, short-eared owl**

and **golden eagle**. This latter is not uncommon amongst the higher hills. **Crows** are also present: some **carrion crows**, but more generally the **hooded crow** (particularly in the west) and the **raven**.

The largest wild mammal in Britain is the **red deer**. These stay high in the hills during the summer – partly to escape the fierce insect life of the summer moors – but return to the lower moors during the winter. There are also local colonies of **sika deer** and **wild goats**. These last (most likely to be seen in Wester Ross) are not truly wild, but are the descendants of domestic animals, although individual herds may be of some antiquity. Carnivores include **wildcat, fox** and **stoat**, while the **mountain hare** – which, like the **ptarmigan** and **stoat** turns white in the winter – can also be found on the moors.

## Seashore *(2,4,7,10,11,16,18,21,24,25,26,27,28,29,30)*

There is an enormous length of coastline in this area, with deep, narrow lochs eating far into the land masses of Skye and Wester Ross, and similarly elongated firths surrounding the Black Isle. In the west, the foreshore is generally of rocks *(2,11,21, 25,26,30)* or cliffs *(25,26,27,28)*, but there are some splendid beaches of sand backed by dunes *(4,7)*, and one fine coral beach on Skye *(24)*.

Rock type and boulder size have some effect on the life of the rocky foreshores, but the most important element is the degree of exposure to heavy seas. On exposed beaches the cover is limited to **lichens** and **barnacles**, while, in the sheltered lochs, there is a greater density of **sea-weeds**, plus **mussels, limpets** and other shellfish. **Crabs** are common between the high and low water marks, while **sea urchins** and **starfish** can be seen just below the lowest tides. The shells of **scallops** and other bivalves are often thrown up along the beaches.

The **common seal** is the sea mammal most likely to be seen; lying on rocky islands and points. In addition, **otters** can sometimes be seen swimming in the sea; particularly in the evening.

Bird life includes a variety of **gulls (herring, common, black-headed, greater black-back** and **kittiwake)** and **terns (common and arctic)**, plus

**fulmar** and **gannet** around the cliffs, along with **razorbill, guillemot, puffin, cormorant** and **shag**. Waders include **curlew, oyster catcher, dunlin, redshank, sandpiper** and others, plus the **heron, mute** (on the southern part of the coast) and **whooper swans**, and **eider, teal, tufted duck, wigeon** and others.

In addition to these, the aerobatics of **ravens** are a feature of many cliff walks, particularly on Skye, while the **sea eagle** – quite recently reintroduced into Scotland on the island of Rum – might possibly be seen.

There are also cliffs along the eastern coast, but the main attractions for birdwatchers in that area are the mud-flats of the Beauly and Cromarty Firths and of Munlochy Bay *(18)*. These attract a great number of waders and ducks including (in addition to those above) **knot, bar-tailed godwit** and **ringed plover; shelduck, pochard, scaup, goldeneye, long-tailed duck, red-breasted merganser, goosander, common scoter** and **mallard**, plus **grey-lag** and **pink-footed geese**.

### Freshwater *(5,6,11,32,)*
There is so much freshwater in this area that it is difficult to avoid it: it drapes itself around the hills as mist and cloud, and falls from the sky in profusion, feeding a multitude of bogs, burns, rivers and marshes. To get home dry is often an accomplishment. Only those routes where a body of water has particular prominence, therefore, are listed above.

The **bog cotton, asphodel** and **myrtle** and various mosses, reeds and grasses of the moors and peat bogs tend to follow the water courses to the sea's edge throughout this area; only being replaced by woodland flowers where the burns pass through high-sided, narrow glens, and trees have been able to grow. Various pondweeds, reeds and sedges grow by the lochs and lochans.

The most impressive of the freshwater birds are the **red-throated** and **black-throated divers**, which nest in the high lochans; specifically chosen for their isolation. Also by the upper waters are **snipe, redshank, greenshank** and **curlew**; while **dipper** and **grey** and **pied wagtails** are quite common by burns and rivers.

There are few mammals which specifically live by the water, but one – the **otter** – is not uncommon throughout the area, although you will be lucky to see one. Other swimmers include **water vole, mink** and **pine marten**.

### Conifer Woodland *(6,8,10,11,12,13,14,15,18,20, 23,32,33,35)*
This heading covers two separate types of woodland: commercial forestry and the remnants of the old Caledonian pine forest *(8)*. The commercial plantations are of comparatively little interest to naturalists. They provide cover for **rabbit, fox, wildcat, pine marten, roe deer** and others, but the trees are generally close together, thus keeping the sunlight from the forest floor and inhibiting the undergrowth necessary to sustain the smaller mammals and insects at the bottom of the food chain. Having said this, there are areas of broad-leaved woodland within most commercial forests, plus open rides between the blocks of trees, and the fact that these areas are within the protection of the parameter fence, and thus relatively free of grazing animals, does help tree regeneration.

The bird life of the plantations can include **blue, great** and **coal tits, bullfinch** and **chaffinch**, plus **crossbill** and **crested tit** in the east of the area. **Redpoll, siskin** and **woodcock** are also present, while the **capercaillie** may also be seen in the east.

The Caledonian pine forest – a relic of the type of woodland which once covered much of the Highlands – is more open, and is comprised of **Scots pine** with a variety of broad-leaved trees and a rich undergrowth of heather and berries. The few remaining areas of this woodland are now protected, and are often fenced off to encourage regeneration.

### Broad-leaved Woodland *(11,12,21,31,32)*
Large stretches of this area are almost totally devoid of trees; felling, grazing and ancient fires having stripped the hills bare. Where patches of broad-leaved woodland remain it tends to be on the steepest slopes, where the grazing sheep and deer cannot reach them; either on the hillsides or in the narrow glens of burns. On the eastern edge of the area a few larger areas of woodland begin to appear.

The type of trees generally encountered are

birch, rowan, hazel, holly and alder, with patches of oak on south-facing slopes. That neither the soil nor the climate make this poverty of trees inevitable is shown by both the success of the famous Inverewe Garden at Poolewe *(5)* and the survival of palm trees in the side streets of Ullapool.

### Farmland *(17,18)*

Over most of the area, farmland means rough grazing land, with cattle being pastured on low, rocky fields, and sheep up onto the moors and hillsides.

In addition there is a certain amount of crofting land. This generally lies in a strip behind the foreshore, and can be quite productive on the low-lying sandy areas of the machair: a band of grazing land, enriched by shell-sand and additionally fertilised by manure and seaweed. The only area of large-scale arable farming is the Black Isle, which is a highly productive agricultural area.

In these areas the wildlife tends to mirror that of the surrounding moors, woodland or foreshore, but there are some birds specific to the fields. **Redwing, fieldfare** and **yellowhammer** throughout the area; **partridge** and **pheasant** in the east and the increasingly rare **corncrake** in the rough grassland and hayfields of the west.

# Advice to Walkers

Always check the weather forecast before setting off on the longer walks and prepare yourself accordingly. Remember that an excess of sunshine – causing sunburn or dehydration – can be just as debilitating as snow or rain, and carry adequate cover for the hills.

Snow cover on the higher slopes often remains well into summer and should be avoided by inexperienced walkers as it often covers hidden watercourses and other pitfalls which are likely to cause injury. Also, when soft, snow is extremely gruelling to cross and can sap the energy very quickly. Walking on snow-covered hills should not be attempted without an ice-axe and crampons.

The other weather-associated danger on the hills is mist or low cloud – particularly common on the West Highland hills – which can appear very swiftly and cut visibility to a few yards. Such conditions should be anticipated, and a map and compass carried while on the higher ground.

Obviously these problems are unlikely to arise on the shorter, simpler routes, but it is always wise when out walking to anticipate the worst and to be ready for it. The extra equipment may never be needed, but it is worth taking anyway, just in case. Spare food, a first-aid kit, a whistle and a torch with a spare battery should be carried on all hill walks. In addition, details of your route and expected time of return should be left with someone, whom you should contact when you return.

There is one final danger for hill walkers which is entirely predictable. From August onwards there is grouse shooting and deer stalking on the moors. If you are undertaking one of the hill routes then check with the local estate or tourist office before doing so, thereby avoiding becoming a nuisance to the sportsmen and risking possible danger to yourself.

### Country Code

All walkers, when leaving public roads to pass through farmland, forestry or moorland, should respect the interests of those whose livelihood depends on the land. Carelessness can easily cause damage. You are therefore urged to follow the Country Code:

   Guard against all risk of fire
   Keep all dogs under proper control
   (especially during the lambing season -
      April/May)
   Fasten all gates
   Keep to the paths across farmland
   Avoid damaging fences, hedges and walls
   Leave no litter
   Safeguard water supplies
   Protect wildlife, wild plants and trees
   Go carefully on country roads
   Respect the life of the countryside

# 1 Stac Pollaidh

**Length:** 2 miles (3km)
**Height climbed:** 1500ft (450m)
**Grade:** B
**Public conveniences:** None
**Public transport:** None

*A short, steep hill climb on rough paths, providing excellent views of moorland and mountain scenery.*

Stac Pollaidh is not particularly high – 2009ft (613m) – but it is one of Scotland's most distinctive hills, with its two craggy summits, linked by a jagged ridge, rising from a steep apron of peat and scree. It is part of the Inverpolly National Nature Reserve, which contains some of the bleakest landscape in the country. The hill rises from an area of damp moorland decorated with a myriad of burns, lochs and lochans, from which emerge a number of other dramatically abrupt peaks.

To reach the start of the climb, drive north from Ullapool on the A835. After around ten miles (16km), turn left onto the unnumbered road signposted for Achiltibuie. After about five miles (8km) there is a car park to the left of the road overlooking Loch Lurgainn, with Stac Pollaidh clearly visible up to the right.

Start up the path directly opposite the car park. The route is clear enough, but the going is tough, damp and treacherous in places. Climb straight up the steep hillside to the lowest point on the ridge (the two peaks should be avoided except by experienced rock climbers). The view from this point is magnificent: northwards across Loch Sionascaig to the peaks of Suilven, Quinaig and Canisp, and (nearer at hand) Cul Mor; southwards to the hills of Coigach.

Drop down the far side of the ridge – the path, once again, is very steep – and follow the cairns around the eastern end of the hill until it rejoins the original track.

While in the neighbourhood, it is worthwhile following the road on along the Coigach peninsula. There are splendid views southwards of the Summer Isles and across the mouth of Loch Broom.

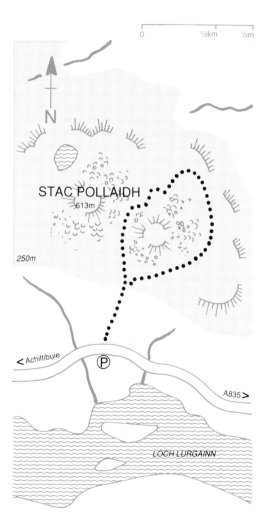

# 2 Rhue Lighthouse

**Length:** 6¹/₂ miles (10.5km)
**Height climbed:** Up to 300ft (90m)
**Grade:** B
**Public conveniences:** Ullapool
**Public transport:** Bus services to Ullapool

*A rough footpath along a rocky foreshore leading to a lighthouse, with an alternative return along the public road. Fine coastal scenery.*

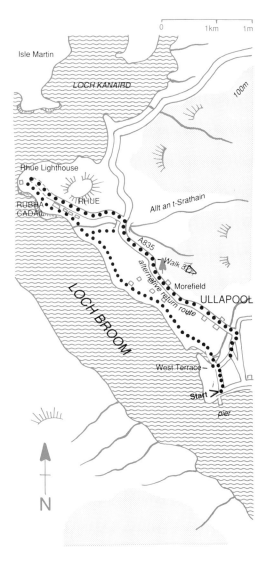

The charming village of Ullapool sits on a spit of land jutting out from the northern shore of Loch Broom, surrounded by splendid mountain and coastal scenery. This is one of the few towns of any size on the west coast and, as the grid-iron arrangement of its central streets makes clear, the original settlement was planned. It was founded in 1788 by the British Fisheries Society, as a base for the herring fishery. The experiment was not an unqualified success, but in more recent years the town has developed into a thriving service centre.

This walk follows the coast out to Rubha Cadail – the northern point at the mouth of Loch Broom – from where there are fine views out towards the Summer Isles and the Coigach peninsula. To start this route, walk along the Ullapool waterfront until the pier for the Stornoway ferry is reached. At this point, turn up into the town and carry straight on to a T-junction. Turn left here, into West Terrace. After a short distance, a flight of steps leads down to the right, into the valley of the Ullapool River. Cross the footbridge over this and then turn sharp left down to the mouth of the river.

Carry on along the shore beyond. The going is easy enough at first, along a grassy verge backed by croft land, but gradually becomes more rocky. After two and a half miles (4km) the mouth of Allt an t-Srathain is reached. Depending on the state of the tide and recent rainfall, this burn may or may not be fordable. If it isn't, climb up its near side to the A835, cross the road bridge, then turn left down the road to Rhue, carrying on to the lighthouse beyond. Otherwise, continue along the foreshore to the same destination.

It is possible to return by the A835, but this can be busy. One alternative is to follow it for about half a mile (1km) then join *Walk 3* – a total distance of around 14 miles (22.5km).

# 3 Loch Achall

**Length:** 4-8 miles (6.5-14km)
**Height climbed:** Up to 600ft (180m) (long route)
**Grade:** B
**Public conveniences:** Ullapool
**Public transport:** Bus service to Ullapool

*A sequence of tracks and footpaths (of varying quality) offering routes of a range of lengths over an area of rough moorland. Excellent views.*

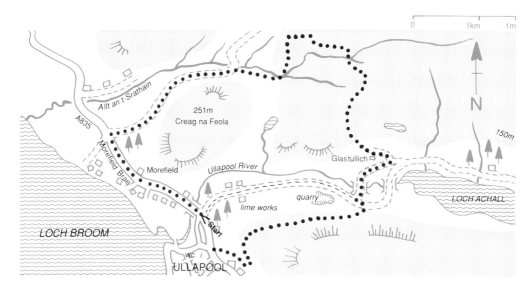

Walk out to the northern end of Ullapool, just before the A835 crosses the Ullapool River. At this point a road heads up the valley of the river. For the shortest variation of this route, walk up this road, past the lime works and quarry (watch out for heavy vehicles on this stretch; also, a red flag is hung by the roadside when blasting is in progress), and join the longer route at the junction to the south of the bridge over the river *(see map)*.

For the longer route, walk north along the A835 (this can be quite busy) for one and a half miles (2.5km) until the top of Morefield Brae is reached. At this point there is a plantation of conifers, beyond which a clear track sets off up the eastern side of the glen of the Allt an t-Srathain. Follow this track until, after one and a half miles (2.5km) it splits, just before crossing the burn. Stay to the right here, fording the burn after a short distance and then continuing along a fainter path.

When the burn splits, keep to the left and follow the path towards a low ridge. Before the crest of the ridge is reached a path cuts off to the right. Follow this as it curves around the headwaters of Allt an t-Srathain, then crosses a low pass and drops down – much clearer now – to Glastullich above Loch Achall.

Carry on down the drive beyond, then turn right at the first junction to cross the bridge over the Ullapool River. For the shorter option at this point, turn right, down the quarry road, back to Ullapool. Otherwise, turn left, and look out for a rough path which soon cuts up to the right and climbs up onto the moorland. From the top of this path there are fine views of Ullapool, Loch Broom and the Summer Isles. Beyond, the path zig-zags down to join the A835, about a quarter of a mile (0.5km) from the start of the walk.

# 4 Mellon Udrigle

**Length:** 3 miles (5km)
**Height climbed:** Undulating
**Grade:** B
**Public conveniences:** None
**Public transport:** None

*A short, low-level circuit through grazing land on clear tracks and quiet public roads, passing both sandy and rocky foreshores and providing fine views of coastal scenery.*

Mellon Udrigle is a tiny, remote township near the tip of one of a sequence of rugged headlands which jut out into the Minch from Wester Ross. Given pleasant weather it is an idyllic spot, with a small number of crofts and cottages spread out along the roadside behind the wide sands of Camas a' Charraig; itself opening out eastwards onto Gruinard Bay (a name now generally associated, sadly, with the contamination of Gruinard Island during the last war).

To reach the route, drive about ten miles (16km) north of Poolewe on the A832. At the small settlement of Laide (by Gruinard Bay) turn westwards onto a minor road and follow it for three miles (5km) until Mellon Udrigle is reached. Park in the car park in the sand dunes behind the beach, then walk on along the road.

After a short distance the road cuts hard right. Turn left onto a clear track, leaving a house to the right. A short way from the road the track splits. Stay right this time, and carry on across the hill, noting the crofts of Opinan lining the hillside to the left.

The track climbs gently for a while, then begins to drop down, with a tidal inlet becoming visible down to the left. If the tide is out, it is possible to cross this inlet by a rough causeway of boulders, just below an area of sand (otherwise see below). Climb up beyond this to join the Opinan road, then follow this back to the start of the route.

Alternatively, a walk of equal length but covering rougher ground can be made by turning right instead of crossing the inlet, and following sheep tracks along the dramatic coastal cliffs and inlets of Rubha Beag; noting the tremendous views to the north of the hills of Coigach and beyond. This sequence of faint paths ends at the northern end of Mellon Udrigle's fine sandy beach.

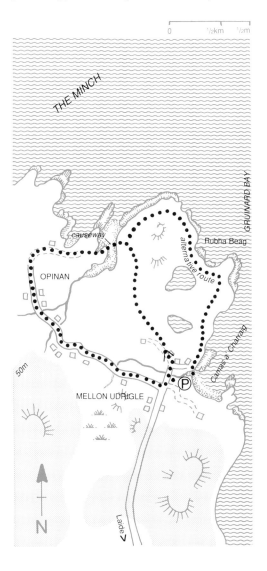

# 5 Poolewe to Fionn Loch

**Length:** Up to 10 miles (16km)
**Height climbed:** Up to 650ft (200m)
**Grade:** A/B/C
**Public conveniences:** Poolewe
**Public transport:** Post bus service between
Achnasheen and Laide (Gruinard Bay)

*A circuit on good tracks and rough footpaths
across an area of moorland. Sections of the
route are by river and lochside, with a
possible extension to a large inland loch.*

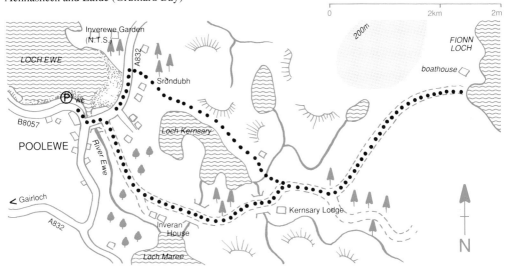

The little village of Poolewe, in Wester Ross, sits at
the sheltered head of Loch Ewe, about five miles
(8km) north of Gairloch along the A832. The
surrounding scenery alone would make the place
worthy of a visit, but there is the added attraction of
Inverewe Garden about a mile (1.5km) to the north
of the village, on a promontory jutting out into the
loch. The garden – first planted in 1862 – is owned
by the National Trust for Scotland.

The footpaths around the garden provide a
pleasant short walk, but for a rather more strenuous
route, drive to Poolewe and turn down the B8057.
There is room for parking almost immediately on
the right.

Walk back to the A832 and turn left over the
bridge, then first right along the road by the side of
the River Ewe (if you want only a short stroll, then
this early, riverside stretch should suffice). When
the road ends, continue along the private road

beyond, towards Inveran House. In an area of
woodland, a little before the house is reached, the
track splits. Take the left-hand track and continue;
across a small river, past the end of Loch Kernsary
and on to Kernsary Lodge.

Once beyond the lodge there is a choice. For
the shorter route, turn left and follow the faint path
– beside Loch Kernsary at first, and then across an
area of moorland – to return to the A832 at
Sròndubh, about half a mile (1km) north of the start
of the route.

For a longer, lineal extension, carry straight on
along a clear track across open moorland to the
boathouse on the edge of Fionn Loch – about five
miles (8km) there and back from Kernsary Lodge,
but well worth the effort on a good day. The view
of the peaks and corries about the southern end of
the loch is tremendous.

Return by the same route.

# 6 Flowerdale Forest

**Length:** Up to 4 miles (6.5km)
**Height climbed:** 650ft (200m) on alternative route
**Grade:** B/C
**Public conveniences:** Gairloch
**Public transport:** Post bus service between
Achnasheen and Laide (along A832)

*A glen walk on good roads and tracks of
varying quality, leading to a pleasant
waterfall. Possible return over rough
moorland.*

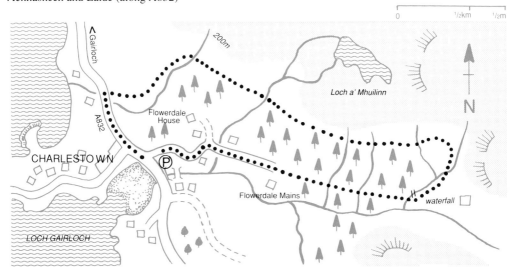

The village of Gairloch, in Wester Ross, sits at the
head of Loch Gairloch, looking westwards towards
the Outer Isles. A mile to the south, along the
A832, is the small harbour of Charlestown, and in
the glen behind sits Flowerdale House (built 1738):
the third residence of the Gairloch MacKenzies to
be built in the glen, the first having been
constructed in the 15th century. At their zenith, at
the end of the 17th century, the MacKenzies were
the most powerful clan in the northern Highlands,
having risen from comparative obscurity to control
vast estates from the Outer Isles in the west to
Cromarty in the east.

At the head of the bay at Charlestown a small
road cuts inland, leaving the A832 immediately to
the north of the bridge over a small river. Turn up
this road and then right again, almost immediately,
into a car park.

Carry on walking along the road; past the front
of Flowerdale House and on, along a metalled road,
to Flowerdale Mains farm. Beyond this the road
becomes rougher and can be very damp when the
weather is wet. It runs through an area of conifers,
by the side of the burn, as far as a small waterfall
near the end of the wood.

Either return by the same route, or (if you feel
the need of some extra exercise) climb up to the left
of the falls and follow a path out of the woodland
and onto the rough moorland of the upper glen
beyond. Turn left, up to the edge of the woodland,
and then follow this back to the road, just north of
Charlestown. This return is harder work, but
provides fine views of the scenery around Loch
Gairloch.

# 7 Red Point to Diabaig

**Length:** 7 miles (11km) one way
**Height climbed:** 450ft (140m)
**Grade:** A
**Public conveniences:** None
**Public transport:** Post bus services: Gairloch to Redpoint; Kinlochewe to Diabaig

*A fine lineal route, clear but rough in places, largely through moorland. Excellent views of surrounding coastal scenery.*

The relatively small number of coastal routes in Wester Ross is not a reflection on the scenery – which is superb – but rather on the fact that the public roads hug so much of the coastline. None the less, there are some good stretches of pathway, of which this route is a fine example. In the nature of these things, this is a lineal route and – unless you plan to return by the same route – transport will have to be arranged for the far end.

The route runs along a stretch of coast on the northern edge of Loch Torridon, with one end of the path at Red Point, at the very mouth of the loch. To reach Red Point, drive three miles (5km) south of Gairloch on the A832, then turn right onto the B8056. This runs some nine miles (14.5km) around the coast before ending at the gate to Redpoint Farm. About a quarter of a mile (0.5km) before this there is a car park by a viewpoint to the right of the road.

Walk down the farm drive, then continue across the sandy fields beyond down to the sand dunes. Turn left, past the huts of the fishing station, then continue along the rough but clear path beyond; crossing a few small burns, but staying close to the coast until the glen of the Craig River is approached. At this point the path turns inland, through an area of birch woodland, to cross a bridge over the river. Beyond this is the Craig Youth Hostel.

Once past the hostel the path climbs onto the shoulder of Sidhean a' Mhill, then continues across rough, damp moorland (the path is vague in places, but marked by cairns) to Lower Diabaig: a cluster of houses by the side of the extraordinary natural amphitheatre of Loch Diabaig.

To start the route from this end, drive some ten miles (16km) south of Kinlochewe to the head of Loch Torridon, along the A896, then turn right onto an unnumbered road. Follow this to its conclusion.

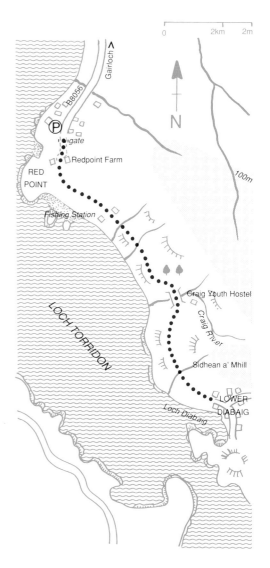

# 8 Beinn Eighe

**Length:** 1-4 miles (1.5-6.5km)
**Height climbed:** Up to 1800ft (550m)
**Grade:** A/C
**Public conveniences:** None
**Public transport:** Post bus service between
Achnasheen and Gairloch

*Steep, rough, dramatic route through Scots
pine woodland and across an exposed rocky
plateau. Tough going in places but wonderful
scenery.* **No dogs.**

Loch Maree is one of the most picturesque of all
Scottish lochs; dotted with wooded islands and
surrounded by high, rugged peaks. Amongst these
is Beinn Eighe, at the southern end of the loch (a
National Nature Reserve, managed by Scottish
Natural Heritage). Two signposted routes have
been established on the lower slopes of the hill: the
shorter route (1 mile/1.5km) exploring the
remaining areas of Scots pine woodland close to
the loch, the longer (4 miles/6.5km) passing
through these and climbing out onto a high plateau.

To reach the start of the route, drive north from
Kinlochewe along the A832. After a little under a
mile (1.5km) there is a visitor centre to the left of
the road, but for this walk continue for a further
two miles (3km) and park in the large car park to
the right of the road.

Start by following the path which passes
beneath the road by the side of a burn.
Immediately beyond the road there is a footbridge
across the burn. For the Woodland Trail walk over
this; for the Mountain Trail carry straight on.

Although the Mountain Trail does not reach the
peaks, it is very steep and (once the trees are left
behind) quite a scramble in places. Also, over the
rough ground it is not always easy to follow the
path, so keep an eye open for the various cairns
which mark the route. Having said this, the views
are spectacular, with the ridge of Beinn Eighe to
the south and a mass of peaks stretching away to
the north and east – notably the dramatic Slioch on
the opposite side of the loch.

Once on the plateau the path passes a couple of
small lochans, then descends, by the side of a deep
gorge, back into the pine forest.

Details of the wildlife and geological features
of this route are provided in a booklet which is
available from the visitor centre. **Please stick to
the path from 1st Sep-15th Feb (deer stalking).**

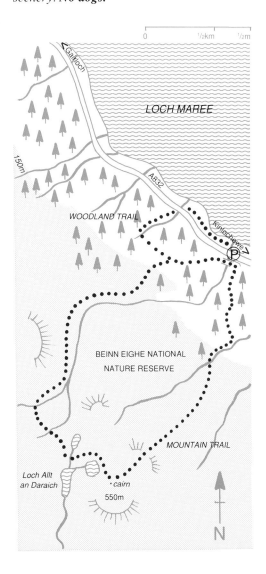

# 9 Coire Mhic Fhearchair

**Length:** 8 miles (13km) there and back
**Height climbed:** 1650ft (500m)
**Grade:** A
**Public conveniences:** None
**Public transport:** Post bus service between
Kinlochewe and Torridon

*A lineal route, on rough paths, leading
through an area of magnificent mountain
scenery to a dramatic corrie. Possible
extensions.*

Around the head of Loch Torridon there is a cluster
of very grand sandstone Munros (peaks over
3000ft). Their narrow ridges and precipitous slopes
make them a Mecca for climbers, while the paths
between them pass through some of the most
majestic mountain scenery to be found in the
Highlands. This particular route follows the
narrow glen between Liathach (3456ft/1054m) and
Beinn Eighe (3217ft/1010m) *(8)*, and leads to one
of the finest conclusions of any walk in this area.

To reach the start of the route, drive six miles
(9.5km) south from Kinlochewe on the A896 road
for Lochcarron. The car park is to the right of the
road, about two miles (3km) after it passes the end
of the wooded Loch Clair, and just at the point
where the burn flowing down the glen on the near
side of Liathach – the vast bulk of which now
becomes visible, ahead and to the right – passes
under the road.

From the car park, start walking by the burn up
into the glen; a long gradual climb during which
the path curves round to the far side of Liathach.
At the watershed at the head of the burn – about
two and a half miles (4km) from the start of the
route – there is a split in the path, marked by a
large cairn. The left-hand path runs for a further
five and a half miles (9km) to the car park near
Torridon House, by the northern shore of Loch
Torridon. For this walk, however, keep right.

The path (which soon becomes faint, but is
marked by a string of cairns) swings round the
rocky lower slopes of Sàil Mhor (the westernmost
peak of Beinn Eighe), above a landscape of wet
moorland divided by abrupt hills, before reaching a
waterfall cascading over a shelf of rock between
the cliffs of Sàil Mhor and Ruadh Stac Mor.
Beyond is a corrie of the most imposing cliffs and
buttresses, at the heart of which is little Loch Coire
Mhic Fhearchair – a sight well worth the climb.

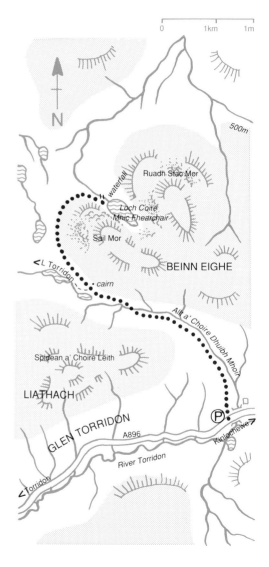

# 10 Leacanashie

**Length:** 4¹/₂ miles (7km)
**Height climbed:** 350ft (100m)
**Grade:** B
**Public conveniences:** None
**Public transport:** None

*A pleasant circuit on rough footpaths, clear tracks and quiet public roads; passing through woodland (largely mature conifer) and offering fine views of coastal scenery.*

To reach the start of this route, turn off the A896 at Lochcarron and follow the narrow coastal road westwards, noting the fine views of the steep, wooded slopes above Stromeferry on the far side of the loch. After a little over three miles (5km) the road reaches the northern pier of the old ferry at Stromemore, with the ruin of Strome Castle (at one time a stronghold of the MacDonnells of Glengarry, but destroyed in 1609) overlooking the pier.

Continue along the Ardaneaskan road for a little under a mile (1.5km) until the road enters an area of woodland and crosses a cattle grid. Park by the road beyond this (if it is not possible to do this without blocking a gateway, continue to the parking place at Ardaneaskan and start the route from there).

A short distance beyond the cattle grid there is a sign for a footpath to Reraig, opposite a small group of houses, with a rough path climbing the hill beyond. Follow this path up to join a clear forest track, and after a short distance turn right (turn marked by a wooden post) onto a smaller path, leading down into the glen of the Reraig Burn through mature conifers.

When the path joins a clear track turn right, and at the next junction turn left, over the bridge across the burn and back down the far side of the glen. This track leaves the woodland and emerges onto the rough grazing land around the head of little Loch Reraig. Follow the track past Reraig Cottage, across the burn, and on along the edge of the tidal inlet, with steep slopes of conifers up to the left. As the track swings round the headland to Ardaneaskan, fine views open up of Applecross, Skye and, across the loch, Plockton *(11)*.

From Ardaneaskan follow the road back, for about a mile (1.5km), to the start of the route.

# 11 Plockton Loop

**Length:** Up to 7 miles (11km)
**Height climbed:** 600ft (180m)
**Grade:** B/C
**Public conveniences:** Plockton
**Public transport:** Post bus service from Kyle of Lochalsh

*A possible circuit, starting on a clear footpath by the shore and continuing through a variety of types of woodland and farmland. Clear tracks and quiet public roads.*

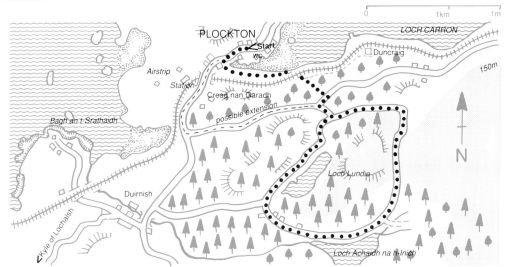

The little village of Plockton is just over five miles (8km) north of Kyle of Lochalsh along minor roads. It is one of the pleasantest settlements on the coast: a couple of streets of small houses and hotels spread along the edge of a shallow, well-protected anchorage. Looking north from the bay there is a fine view of the islands and rocky, wooded headlands around the mouth of Loch Carron, with the dramatic mountain scenery of Wester Ross visible beyond.

For this route, walk south from the centre of the village. When the bay ends to the left, there is a signpost for a footpath to Duncraig. Turn left onto this and follow it around the head of the bay, and then on between the railway line and the shore. There are fine views of the village and its anchorage from this stretch of path.

After a short way the path ducks under the railway line and starts to climb the wooded hill behind. A path cuts off to the left (to Duncraig); ignore this and carry on, climbing gently through the trees to join a quiet public road.

Turn right along the road to reach a junction. For a short route, turn right and follow the public road two and a half miles (4km) back to Plockton. For a longer walk, turn left, then left again at the next junction, and follow a narrow road through mixed woodland in a loop of a little under four miles (6.5km). Keep to the right at each junction, passing Loch Achaidh na h-Inich and Loch Lundie along the way; pleasantly situated amongst tree-covered hills. Be careful to shut the forestry gates behind you.

When the loop is complete, return either by the original path or by the alternative route along the public road previously mentioned.

# 12 Balmacara Forest Walk

**Length:** 2-4 miles (3-6.5km)
**Height climbed:** 400ft (120m)
**Grade:** B
**Public conveniences:** None
**Public transport:** None

*Two fine forest walks on clear, signposted paths; passing through both conifer and broad-leaved woodland, and providing excellent views (particularly from the longer route).*

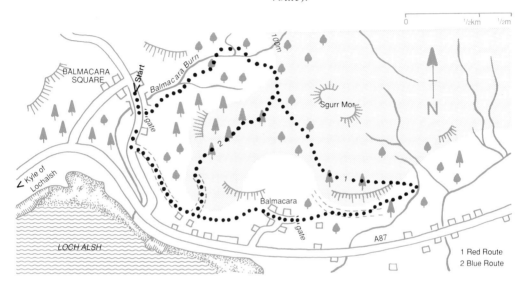

These two routes start from the little village of Balmacara Square, in a valley to the north of Loch Alsh. To reach it, drive three miles (5km) east of Kyle of Lochalsh on the A87, then turn left onto a minor road.

Park in the village then walk south on the eastern exit road. After a short distance the road crosses the Balmacara Burn, and just beyond this there is a gate to the left signposted for the 'forest walk'. Follow this path along the burn side, with the slopes of Sgurr Mor visible ahead, until it enters the conifer plantation and begins a steep ascent. Once the climb has levelled out the path crosses the burn, then recrosses it, before climbing up to join a clear track. Turn right along this.

After a short distance a smaller path cuts off from the main track (just before it enters an area of beech woodland). For the shorter (blue) route,

continue down the main track; for the longer (red) route take the higher path, leading on along the slope of the hill, the trees gradually clearing to allow wonderful views of Loch Alsh, the narrow sound of Kyle Rhea and the surrounding hills of Skye and the mainland.

The path continues round the hill until it reaches a burn flowing down the slope through an area of oakwood, at which point it drops down to join a clear track. Turn right and at the first junction keep to the left (there is a post indicating the route). Shortly after this a gate is reached, beyond which a road continues in front of a house. Continue to the next house, then join a rougher path which continues through an area of gorse. At the next junction (at which the shorter route rejoins) carry straight on, back to the public road. Turn right to return to Balmacara Square.

# 13 Falls of Glomach

**Length:** 10-12 miles (16-19km)
**Height climbed:** 1650ft (500m)
**Grade:** A
**Public conveniences:** None
**Public transport:** None

*A long, steep lineal route on clear tracks through forestry and across fine open moorland, leading to a dramatic waterfall. Possible alternative return route on rougher paths.*

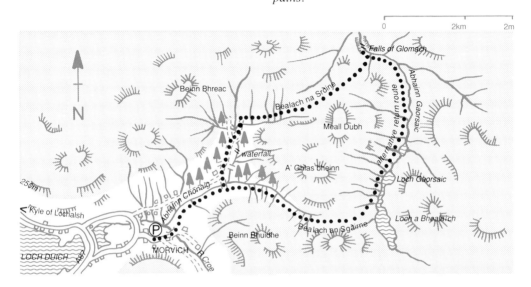

The Falls of Glomach – including a sheer fall of around 300 ft (90m) – are among the highest in the British Isles and provide a spectacular culmination to this fine moorland walk.

To reach the start of the route, drive 14 miles (22.5km) east of Kyle of Lochalsh on the A87 and, at the head of Loch Duich, turn left up the single-track road signposted for Morvich. Park at the Kintail Countryside Centre and then walk on along the metalled road beyond before crossing the River Croe and following a rough, damp, signposted path to a footbridge over the Abhainn Chonaig. At the top of the far bank turn right along a clear path which quickly joins a Forestry Commission track. Follow the signs for 'Glomach Falls' from this point to reach the edge of the plantation.

Ahead, a path is visible zig-zagging up the slope to the left of a steep glen. Follow this up to Bealach na Sròine, then down across the moor

beyond to the top of the falls. There is a tortuous path by the side of the falls, leading to a viewpoint about half way down. It is well worth the effort, and the way is not as dangerous as it appears from above, though a great deal of care must still be taken.

For the shorter walk, return by the same route. For those wishing a little variety, however, there is an alternative. Walk back up the near bank of the Abhainn Gaorsaic to a succession of small lochs in the mountainous upper part of the glen. There is no clear path, but, although the going is rough in places amongst the peat hags, the route is never in doubt.

From Loch Gaorsaic a clear track is visible climbing up the slope to the right. Follow this up into the rocky Bealach an Sgàirne, then on down the dramatic glen beyond; the narrow path edging along a steep slope high above the tiny burn.

This path rejoins the original route a little before the footbridge over the Abhainn Chonaig.

# 14 Fyrish Monument

**Length:** 4 miles (6.5km) there and back
**Height climbed:** 900ft (270m)
**Grade:** B
**Public conveniences:** None
**Public transport:** None

*A moderate climb through an area of mixed woodland, leading to a large monument on a clear summit. Fine views across the Cromarty Firth.*

One of the most distinctive landmarks in the area is the Fyrish Monument – situated at the summit of the conifer-covered Cnoc Fyrish, overlooking the southern shore of Easter Ross and the Cromarty Firth beyond. It takes the form of the wall of an Indian temple and was the idea of General Sir Hector Munro of Novar (1726-1805) (Novar is the estate to the south of the hill), who built it as a job creation scheme for the unemployed locals. There is now a good track up the hill, and the views from the monument are excellent.

To reach the start of the walk, drive some 19 miles (30.5km) north of Inverness on the A9: across the Kessock Bridge and the Cromarty Firth, and on until, a short distance after by-passing Evanton, the A836 cuts off to the left. Turn onto this road and follow it for about two miles (3km) until a minor road cuts off to the left signposted for Boath. Follow this for a little over a mile. Just after the conifers start to the left there is a car park.

Go through the gate at the back of the car park and follow the clear track beyond as it climbs through pleasant woodland, largely of conifers. As the track nears the summit it emerges onto open moorland. From the monument there are excellent views of the entire length of the Cromarty Firth and south to the Black Isle.

While in the area it is worth making a diversion to look at the Black Rock Gorge of the River Glass. To reach it, drive back to Evanton (see above) and look for the minor road following the northern side of the river. A short distance up this road there is an entrance into the area of dense woodland to the left of the road, and beyond this a footpath leading to the gorge – the foot of the gorge is little over a mile (1.5km) from the centre of Evanton. At its most exaggerated point, the gorge is less than 20ft/6m wide, and over 100ft/30m deep.

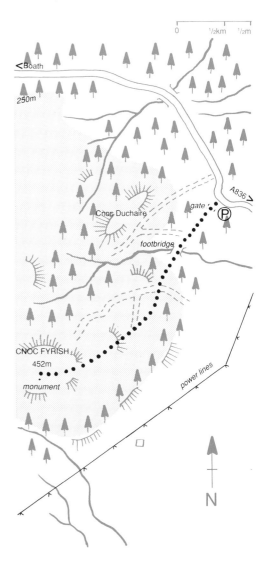

# 15 Knock Farrel

**Length:** 1/2-4 miles (1-6km) there and back
**Height climbed:** 350ft (90m)
**Grade:** B/C
**Public conveniences:** Strathpeffer
**Public transport:** None

*Two short, well-signposted routes through an area of forestry, plus a longer walk leading onto an open hill. Fine views.*

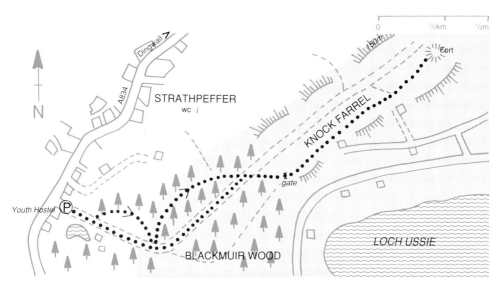

Strathpeffer – four miles (6.5km) west of Dingwall on the A834 – is an old spa village, set in a hilly country of farmland and forestry. The springs first became an attraction in the 18th century, but the village did not develop as a resort until the Victorian period. Nowadays it is a popular tourist centre.

To the south of the village is Knock Farrel: a long, low hill, half covered by forestry, the ridge of which provides fine views over the surrounding countryside. The longest of these routes follows the ridge of the hill.

To reach the start of the routes, drive south from the centre of the village, watching for the Youth Hostel to the left of the road. Turn left up the road immediately before the hostel. A short way along this road there is a car park.

The two shorter, signposted routes (half a mile/1km and two miles/3km) stick to the forestry. All three start in the same way, but the shorter routes quickly double back along a clear track *(see map)*. The longest route crosses this clear track, then continues to a gate at the edge of the forestry. Continue along the undulating ridge of the hill beyond, crossing a track which runs through a dip in the hill and climbing up beyond to reach the grassy mounds of an old Iron Age fort on a low summit. The view from this point is fine: east to Dingwall, north to Ben Wyvis (3433ft/1046m), west to Strathpeffer and south across Loch Ussie.

Return by the same route until the clear track through the forestry is reached, then turn left down that to return to the start.

# 16 Chanonry Point

**Length:** 4 miles (6.5km)
**Height climbed:** Negligible
**Grade:** C
**Public conveniences:** Fortrose
**Public transport:** Bus service from Inverness

*A low-level circuit on public roads, grass tracks and a sandy foreshore, passing the ruins of Fortrose Cathedral and providing fine views of coastal scenery.*

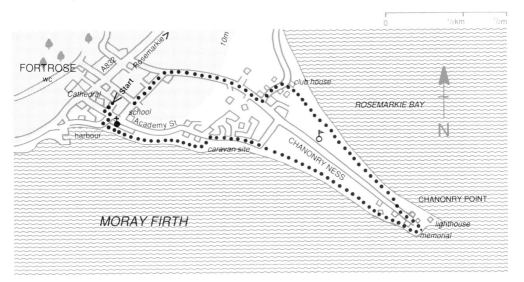

The old royal burgh of Fortrose is a quiet town on the eastern side of the Black Isle, overlooking the Moray Firth. It sits at the landward end of Chanonry Ness – a low, narrow promontory, jutting out into the firth towards a similar projection from the southern shore. This route runs out to the end of the promontory.

To reach Fortrose, drive north from Inverness along the A9. Two miles (3km) beyond the Kessock Bridge turn right, onto the B9161 for Munlochy. When this road joins the A832 turn right for about five miles (8km) to reach Fortrose.

Park in Cathedral Square (noting the ruin of the 13th/15th century cathedral) and start walking along Academy Street. Just before the church, turn right into St Andrew's Walk, heading down towards the harbour. Before this is reached, turn left along the shore and follow it as far as the caravan site (at high tide this stretch can be

blocked, in which case simply follow Academy Street to the site), then turn up to the left to join the metalled road running through the site. When this road cuts hard left, carry straight on along a grass track.

Follow this, along the edge of a golf course, to the end of the promontory, from where there are fine views down the firth in both directions, and across the narrows to Fort George (mid 18th century). Note also the memorial to the Brahan Seer (the famous soothsayer), who was reputedly burned on Chanonry Point.

From the lighthouse, walk a short distance back up the road, then turn right along a marked path down to the shore. Turn left along the sandy foreshore until the golf clubhouse appears to the left. Climb up to the car park and turn left along the road beyond. Turn right at the junction to return to Fortrose.

# 17 Fortrose to Avoch

**Length:** 4¹/₂ miles (7km)
**Height climbed:** 250ft (70m)
**Grade:** B
**Public conveniences:** Fortrose, Avoch
**Public transport:** Bus service from Inverness

*A low-level circuit along quiet public roads and the route of a disused railway, passing through a mixture of farmland and woodland. Fine views over the Moray Firth.*

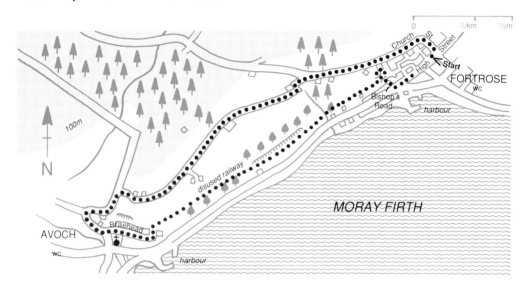

Start this route in Fortrose, the old royal burgh on the eastern side of the Black Isle. To reach the town, drive north from Inverness on the A9. Two miles (3km) north of the Kessock Bridge turn right on to the B9161. At Munlochy, turn right onto the A832 and follow it for five miles (8km) to Fortrose.

Park in the centre and walk up Church Street, off the High Street. Follow this road along the edge of the town until, just after the last of the houses, a small road cuts off to the left. Turn down this and follow it through an area of farmland, noting the fine views to the left across the Moray Firth and ahead to the fishing village of Avoch. When the road reaches a T-junction turn left; when another road joins from the right, continue to swing round to the left.

Turn left up a road called Braehead; passing a prominent church and then continuing. At the end of the road turn left, up a track beside a house, then climb up to join the bed of the old Fortrose-Avoch railway. Follow this back to Fortrose, through woodland and farmland.

As the line reaches the edge of Fortrose it crosses a road by a small bridge. At the end of the bridge there are some steps leading down to this road (Bishop's Road). Drop down here and turn left, under the railway line, to return to the High Street near the west end of the town.

While on the Black Isle, it is worth driving the extra ten miles (16km) out to the fine old town of Cromarty on the tip of the peninsula.

# 18 Munlochy Bay

**Length:** 2¹/₂-5 miles (4-8km)
**Height climbed:** 260ft (80m)
**Grade:** B/C
**Public conveniences:** Avoch
**Public transport:** Bus service from Inverness

*A low-level circuit (with possible shorter alternative) through mixed woodland and farmland, passing mud-flats rich in bird life. Public roads and clear tracks.*

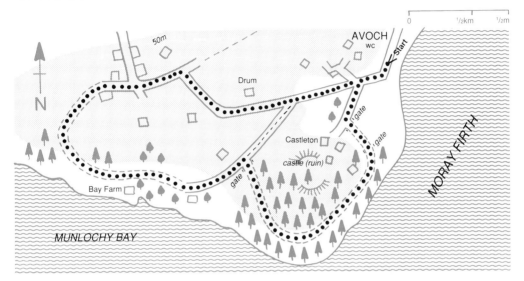

Munlochy Bay is a muddy, tidal inlet, biting about two miles (3km) into the eastern coast of the Black Isle from the Moray Firth. It is an excellent place for spotting duck, geese and waders and is now listed as a nature reserve. This route does not go down to the side of the bay, but looks down on it from a track along its northern side.

The route starts at the little fishing village of Avoch. To reach this, drive north from Inverness on the A9. Two miles (3km) beyond the Kessock Bridge, turn right onto the B9161. At Munlochy (at the head of the bay) turn right along the A832 for a little over three miles (5km). Once in the village, turn right along the waterfront road and park near the end of the houses.

Continue walking beyond, along a narrow road which climbs inland. After a short distance, turn left up the driveway to Castleton. Shortly before the farm is reached, turn left through a gate and follow a grassy track to a gate leading into a conifer plantation. Follow the clear track beyond this through the trees, noting the ruins of Ormond Castle on a low mound to the right. This is thought to have been the stronghold of Andrew de Moray – one of the leaders of William Wallace's Scottish army at the Battle of Stirling Bridge (1297).

Follow this track out of the trees and on to a junction with a narrow public road. For the shorter route, turn right, then right again at the next junction, to return to Avoch. For the longer route, turn left, and follow a pleasant road (metalled, but of gradually deteriorating quality) through an area of farmland and mixed woodland along the slope above Munlochy Bay.

Continue along this road as it turns inland. At the first junction carry straight on, along a quiet public road. At the second continue along this road (ie, turn hard right), then carry on through open farmland back to Avoch.

# 19 Quiraing

**Length:** 4 miles (6.5km)
**Height climbed:** 950ft (290m)
**Grade:** A
**Public conveniences:** None
**Public transport:** None

*A series of rough paths through an area of soaring cliffs and extraordinary rock formations. Tough going in places but extremely dramatic.*

Quiraing (Norse for the 'Ridge of the Fold') provides one of the most dramatic areas of geological formations to be found in Skye – rivalled only by the Old Man of Storr *(20)*, about 11 miles (18km) south along the ridge of Trotternish. To reach it, drive some 19 miles (30km) north of Portree on the A855. From Brogaig, just north of Staffin, turn left on to the single-track road to Uig. Follow this for around two and a half miles (4km) and, just after the road has zig-zagged up the face of the ridge, park in the car park to the left of the road.

Start walking opposite the car park, and follow a rough but clear track which runs along the base of the cliffs, with a steep grassy slope dropping down to the right, and isolated rocky hills emerging from the grass on the far side of a rough valley. The most imposing of these is The Prison: a huge, tilted square block. Level with the northern end of this block, a shaft of rock about 120ft (40m) high, called The Needle, rises amongst the towering cliffs to the left of the path. (A rough scramble up the narrow gully to the left of this leads up to The Table: a patch of flat grassland high amongst the imposing buttresses of the cliffs. This detour adds to the distances shown above.)

Continue along the path beneath the foot of the cliffs: past a small lochan to the right and through a gap in a stone dyke, noting the knot of peaks and ridges visible ahead. When the ridge to the left reaches its lowest point, climb up on to it, then turn left again, back along the top of the cliffs (taking all due care). The initial climb up the slopes of Meall na Suiramach is gruelling, but the views (including a spectacular one down onto The Table from above) are magnificent.

After a little over a mile (1.5km) the car park becomes visible ahead.

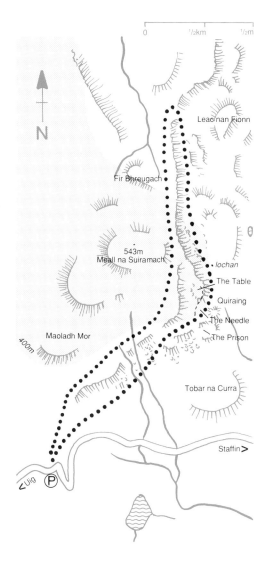

# 20 *Old Man of Storr*

**Length:** 3¹/₂ miles (5.5km)
**Height climbed:** 1000ft (300m)
**Grade:** B
**Public conveniences:** None
**Public transport:** Bus service between Portree and Staffin

*A short, steep climb on rough tracks to an area of extraordinary and precipitous rock formations. Wonderful scenery; some care and sure-footedness required.*

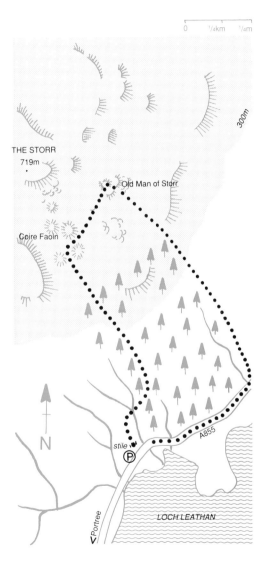

On an island rich in dramatic scenery, perhaps the most dramatic sight of all is the Old Man of Storr: a sheer pinnacle of rock, 160ft (49m) high, standing beneath the steep cliffs of The Storr (2360ft/719m). This famous geological curiosity is on the eastern side of the Trotternish peninsula, and can be reached by driving a little over six miles (9.5km) north from Portree on the A855 road for Staffin. Watch for the cliffs ahead and to the left, and park just before the start of a conifer plantation to the left of the road, near the northern end of Loch Leathan.

Cross a stile over the fence by the road, and walk up the slope beyond, with a dyke to the right and the plantation beyond that. The Old Man of Storr is visible ahead, with the buttresses of the Storr behind it, and a long line of cliffs sweeping away to the left. About half way up the edge of the plantation the path veers right, into the trees, and continues. It can be very wet under foot at this point.

Climb to the upper edge of the trees and look up the steep, grassy slope beyond. Beneath the massive cliffs there are two craggy protuberances like broken gateposts emerging from the grass. Start up the slope and aim to pass between them. The path is a steep one, but it is worth the effort, for once through the gap the route enters an area of extraordinary geological contortions. There are a number of paths beyond. Follow (carefully) whichever you prefer, through the cliffs and boulders, until the base of the Old Man is reached.

From this point there are splendid views across the Sound of Raasay, and south to the hills of southern Skye. The plantation is visible below, with a clear path running down to its left-hand edge. Follow this down to the road, then turn right to return to the start.

# 21 Portree Loop

**Length:** 2½ miles (4km)
**Height climbed:** 400ft (120m)
**Grade:** B
**Public conveniences:** Portree
**Public transport:** Numerous bus services to
Portree

*A short loop on rough paths (which can be
damp in places) through grazing land and
woodland and along a rocky foreshore. Fine
coastal scenery.*

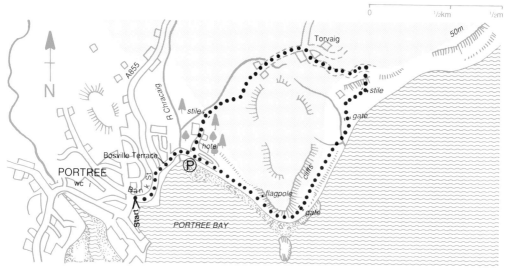

Portree is the administrative centre for Skye: a
small, tight knit town clustered about a sheltered
bay. The name means 'King's Harbour' – a
reference to a visit paid to the island by King
James V in 1540 – although the town itself was not
developed until the 19th century.

This route leads out around the headland to the
north of the bay, and starts from the town centre.
Walk north up Bank Street, then turn right along
the curving Bosville Terrace, from where there are
fine views down into the busy anchorage. Keep
right at the next two junctions, swinging east along
the northern shore of the bay. Just after passing a
parking area to the right, there is a split: the road
heading off ahead left, the path (signposted 'jetty')
continuing by the bay.

The path is quite clear at this point, and remains
so as far as the viewpoint and flagpole
(commemorating the association of the Nicolson

clan with the area), but becomes rougher beyond,
as it swings round the steep headland.

Just beyond the point there is a gate in a dyke.
Go through this and continue across damp
grassland, with a fence to the right, until another
fence crosses the way. Turn left along this until a
gate is reached; go through this and continue
around the edge of the field beyond. At the top of
the field there is a stile. Cross this and climb up the
slope beyond before turning left along a clear track,
climbing to the top of the hill.

When the track reaches the houses at Torvaig,
take the track beyond the house to the left, heading
down towards two large farm buildings. Pass
between these and then continue across rough
moorland, with Portree visible in the valley ahead.

Cross a stile as the path enters an area of
woodland, then continue downhill, passing to the
right of a hotel, before rejoining the original road
near the car park.

# 22 *Waternish Point*

**Length:** 8 miles (13km) there and back
**Height climbed:** Negligible
**Grade:** A
**Public conveniences:** None
**Public transport:** None

*A clear lineal track through an area of rough grazing and moorland, leading to a ruined township. Fine views of coastal scenery.*

This walk starts at the car park opposite the ruin of Trumpan Church, near the end of the Waternish peninsula. The church seems a peaceful spot now, but in 1578 it was the scene of a notorious atrocity, when a party of MacDonalds from Uist barred the door and set fire to the roof thatch with the congregation still inside. The raiders themselves were subsequently killed by a vengeful party of MacLeods.

To reach the church, drive three miles (5km) north of Dunvegan on the A850, then turn left onto the B886 road. Follow this until it turns down to the shore at Lusta, at which point a single-track road cuts right. Follow this for a further four miles (6.5km), ignoring the roads cutting off to the right, until the church is reached on a low hill overlooking the Minch.

From the car park, walk on along a straight section of road. When this turns right at a right angle, turn left, through a gate and on along a clear track (no dogs allowed, please note). Follow this track through a field, through another gate, then on across an area of rough grazing and moorland. The track is good and the route is never in doubt.

Apart from the tremendous views westwards, across the Minch to the Outer Isles, there are a number of points of interest along the way. The first is a monument, to the left of the track, commemorating Roderick MacLeod of Unish, who died hereabouts in battle with the MacDonalds of Trotternish in around 1530. A short distance beyond, to the right of the track, is the first of two brochs (Iron Age defensive structures) visible from the route. The second is a little under a mile (1.5km) further on. At the end of the track there are a number of ruins, including one of a substantial two storey house. Beyond these, an extra walk of two miles (3km) (there and back) leads to the lighthouse on Waternish Point.

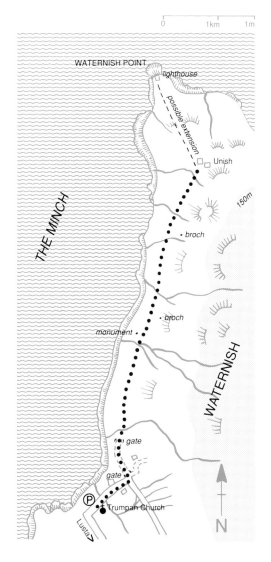

# 23 Waternish Loop

**Length:** 4-5 miles (6.5-8km)
**Height climbed:** 250ft (70m), undulating
**Grade:** B
**Public conveniences:** None
**Public transport:** Post bus service from Dunvegan
to Gillen

*A circuit on clear tracks and quiet public
roads, through grazing land, moorland and
conifer forestry. Fine views of coastal
scenery.*

To reach the Waternish peninsula, drive three miles
(5km) north of Dunvegan on the A850, then turn
left onto the B886. Follow this for four miles
(6.5km) until it begins to turn down to the
waterfront just beyond Lusta. At this point take the
unnumbered road which cuts off to the right.

After a short distance the road enters a narrow
band of woodland above Waternish House. One
end of this route starts to the right of the road at this
point, from a wide gateway beside a burn. If there
is room, park by the side of this gateway; if it is not
possible to do this without blocking the entrance
then carry on until a convenient spot presents itself.
If you are doing the whole circuit it is unimportant
where you park, but if you are only doing the hill
track, continue until the road for Gillen cuts off to
the right. Follow this until it reaches a T-junction
then turn right again. There is room to park at the
end of the road.

Starting from the gate above Waternish House,
walk up the clear track beyond, with grassland to
either side. As the track climbs, the views to the
south, of the islands and headlands around the
mouth of Loch Dunvegan, begin to open up.

Continue along the track, by the left-hand edge
of a stand of conifers (ignoring a track which cuts
off to the right), then through the trees for a short
distance before emerging on the far side of the hill.
There are fine views ahead of Loch Snizort and the
little Ascrib Islands, with the peninsula of
Trotternish beyond.

A short distance beyond the trees the track
splits. The right-hand track leads down to the shore
of Loch Losait, while the left-hand track leads to
the road end at Gillen. From this point either return
by the same route or else follow the quiet public
road back to the start.

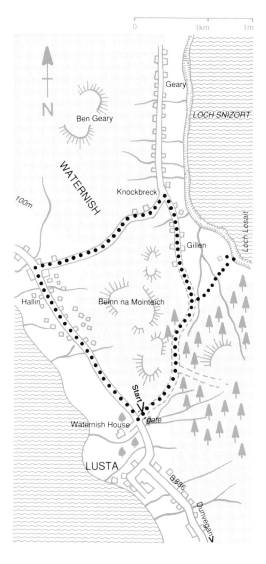

# 24 Coral Beaches

**Length:** 2 miles (3km)
**Height climbed:** Negligible
**Grade:** C
**Public conveniences:** None
**Public transport:** Bus service from Portree to Dunvegan Castle

*A short lineal route through rough grazing land and by a rocky foreshore, leading to a fine shell and coral beach.*

The Coral Beaches are unusual in being composed not of sand, but of a mixture of shell particles and tiny pieces of calcified seaweed. This produces a foreshore of a pale ochre colour, which turns to a fine turquoise when seen through the water at high tide.

To reach the beaches, drive to Dunvegan, then turn north along the A850 for a mile (1.5km) to the entrance to Dunvegan Castle: the seat of the Chiefs of the MacLeods. Traditions dating parts of the structure back to the 9th century are open to question, but there is no doubt that the MacLeods were in residence at least as early as the 14th century. This makes Dunvegan the oldest castle in Britain known to have been continuously inhabited by the same family. It is now open to the public and is well worth a visit while you are in the area.

Beyond the castle the road becomes single-track and continues for another four miles (6.5km) with Loch Dunvegan to the left. When the road reaches a T-junction at Claigan (near its conclusion), turn left, into a car park.

Walk through the gate at the far end of the car park (please note: no dogs allowed) and continue along the clear track beyond through an area of rough grazing. Pass through another gate (noting the sign warning about the bull) and continue along the track, which now runs behind the shore. After a short way a low ridge cuts across the route. Climb over this and continue along the rough footpath beyond to the Coral Beaches, backed by a pleasant area of cropped grassland.

From the end of the headland, beyond the beaches, there are fine views of the little islands of Isay, Mingay and Clett, near the mouth of the loch, and of the Waternish peninsula beyond *(22,23)*.

Return by the same route.

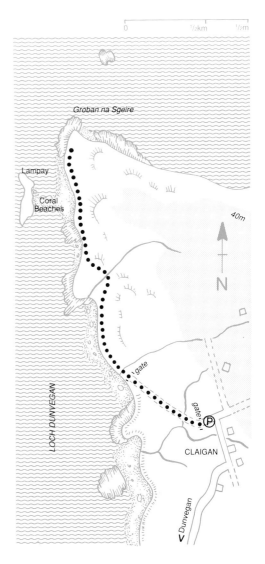

Walk 24

# 25 Neist Point

**Length:** 1¹/₂ miles (2.5km) there and back
**Height climbed:** 300ft (90m)
**Grade:** C
**Public conveniences:** None
**Public transport:** None

*A short lineal route, undulating steeply, leading out to a lighthouse on an exposed cape. Clear paths and wonderful views of surrounding sea cliffs.*

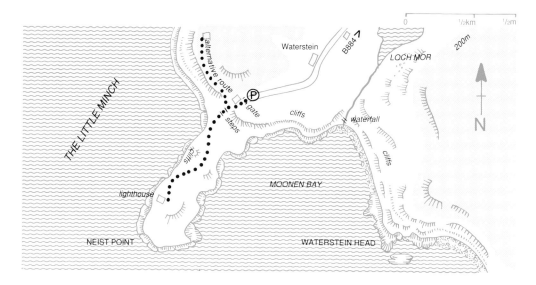

The Neist Point lighthouse is the most westerly on Skye, and it occupies a dramatic position on a narrow, grassy headland jutting out from a coastline of high cliffs. The short walk to the lighthouse is one of the pleasantest on the island.

To reach Neist Point, drive south from Dunvegan on the A863 for about a mile (1.5km), then turn right onto the B884. Follow this road (ignoring the numerous turns to right and left) for about nine miles (14.5km) until a road turns off to the left for Waterstein. Follow this for a little over two miles (3km) until the end of the road is reached. At this point there is a car park.

Go through the gate at the end of the car park and down the steep flight of steps beyond, leading down into the narrow neck of the headland. Looking to the left, there is a fine view of the tall

cliffs of Waterstein Head, with a dramatic waterfall cascading down the lower cliffs beyond, while ahead are the cliffs on the northern side of Neist Point. This is a splendid place for birdwatching, with fulmars, gannets and ravens all likely to be seen.

From the low neck the path climbs again, leaving the highest part of the headland to the right, then drops back down towards the lighthouse – 62ft (19m), built in 1909 and now unmanned. Allow some time to explore the headland beyond the lighthouse, noting the fine views westwards to the Outer Isles, before returning by the same route.

From the car park there is an alternative, shorter route, out along the cliff-tops to the north. This walk provides a good view down to the lighthouse.

Walk 25

# 26 Oronsay

**Length:** 3 miles (5km) there and back
**Height climbed:** Up to 250ft (70m), undulating
**Grade:** C
**Public conveniences:** None
**Public transport:** None

*A short, lineal route through rough grazing
land to a small, grassy island (cut off at high
tide). Paths can be wet, but fine sea cliffs and
coastal scenery.*

The name 'Oronsay' – quite common in the
Scottish islands – is of Norse origin, and means
'tidal island'. This particular Oronsay remaining
true to its name, **it is important to check the state
of the tide before crossing.** The tidal section of
the route is only short, and the island itself small
enough to be crossed in a few minutes, but there is
no point in risking becoming cut off.

To reach the route, drive nine miles (15km)
south of Dunvegan on the A863, then turn right on
the single-track road signposted for Ullinish. After
a little under two miles (3km), park near the hotel.
Go through a gate between the buildings opposite
the hotel and follow the path beyond until the
remains of a building appear to the left. Turn left,
across an open area, to a small gate leading on to a
metalled road. Turn right and follow this until a
gate is reached to the right of the road, just before
the last house.

Go through the gate and continue along a clear
track. When a bay comes in from the left there is a
second gate, beyond which the path becomes
narrower, and can be very damp, but remains clear.
Follow this to a further gate, near the end of the
headland, beyond which the rough path drops down
through a gully to the causeway of loose stones
leading across to the island.

There are no buildings on the island, but the
cropped grass provides pleasant walking, and there
are dramatic cliffs around the western end. To get
the best views around Loch Bracadale, climb up to
the highest point (being careful when approaching
the summit as the cliffs drop sheer immediately
beyond). To the west is Wiay, and the smaller
Harlosh and Tarner Islands, with Idrigill Point and
Macleod's Maidens beyond. To the east is the
lighthouse on Ardtreck Point, at the mouth of Loch
Harport, while to the south the cottages of
Fiskavaig are visible above the low cliffs *(27)*.

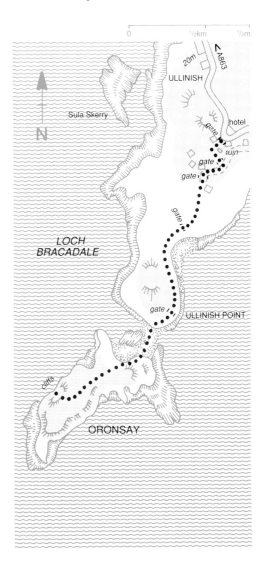

# 27 Talisker

**Length:** 5¹/₂ miles (9km)
**Height climbed:** 400ft (120m), undulating
**Grade:** B
**Public conveniences:** None
**Public transport:** Bus service between Portree and Fiskavaig

*A pleasant route on clear tracks; through rough grazing land at first and leading to a wide bay flanked by sea cliffs.*

To reach the start of this route, drive five miles (8km) west of Sligachan on the A863, then turn left on the B8009. From Portnalong, turn left onto the road signposted for Fiskavaig. Some three miles (5km) along this road there is a severe hairpin bend. Look for a space to park here (being careful not to block any gateways).

Go through the gate by the hairpin and start walking along the track beyond; leading southwards through the rough grazing land of a shallow valley, with peat cuttings down to the left of the track. As the track continues, the rocky mass of Preshal More – looking a little like the half-eroded Sphinx in the Valley of the Kings – becomes clearer on the far side of Gleann Oraid.

After a little over a mile (1.5km) the track zig-zags down into the valley beside a waterfall. At the foot of the slope there is a cottage. Pass to the right of this and continue along the clear track beyond; through a farm and on to a metalled road. Two roads cut off to the right. Ignore the right-hand one (a private entrance to Talisker House) and take the other; with a steep slope to the left and a wall to the right with deciduous woodland beyond.

The track passes Talisker House and crosses a burn, immediately beyond which there is a sign to the right, indicating the 'scenic walk to the sea', and a gate. Go through and follow a clear path by the side of the burn, flanked by trees and meadows full of wild flowers, down to the stony beach at the head of Talisker Bay. From here there are fine views of the great sea-cliffs to the north and south. Note the splendid waterfall cascading down the cliffs to the north of the bay.

Turn left along the shore to join a clear track which leads back up to Talisker House, then return by the original route.

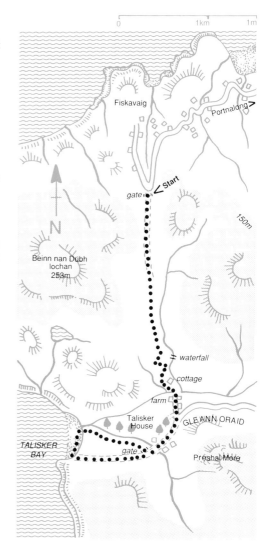

# 28 Glenbrittle

**Length:** 6 miles (9.5km) there and back
**Height climbed:** Undulating
**Grade:** A
**Public conveniences:** Camp site
**Public transport:** None

*A long, lineal route on rough paths across rugged grazing land. Some navigation required when paths peter out at far end of route. Fine coastal scenery.*

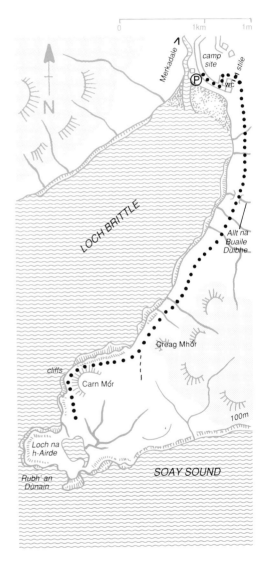

Glen Brittle curves around the western edge of the Cuillin Hills, and the car park at the point where the river empties into Loch Brittle is a favoured starting point for many of the routes through this dramatic range. These routes require some climbing experience, however, and none are described in this guide (those who are interested in the hill routes can obtain details locally). It is not necessary to take to the hills in order to find good walking, however, and there is a very pleasant coastal route running southwards from the car park towards the headland of Rubh' an Dùnain.

To reach the start of the route, drive west from Sligachan on the A863. After six miles (9.5km) the B8009 cuts off to the left. Follow this for about two miles (3km) to Merkadale, then turn left again on the unnumbered road for Glenbrittle. After about eight miles (13km) the road reaches the camp site at the head of Loch Brittle. Park in the spaces by the road and walk on into the camp site. Look for the public conveniences to the right of the road and walk down to the left of them, then cross the stile over the fence beyond. Two paths head off to the right – they run parallel, so either will do.

Continue along the slope above the loch. The ground can be very wet, and some agility may be required to cross the various burns which flow down the slope towards Loch Brittle, but the largest of these (Allt na Buaile Duibhe) does have a bridge across it.

After two and a half miles (4km) the path climbs up and around the shoulder of Creag Mhór. From this point there are views of the islands of Rum and Canna, while the rough path can be seen to split in the low ground beyond the hill. Either path will lead on down to Loch na h-Airde, but the right-hand route, along the cliff edge beneath Carn Mór, is drier, clearer and more dramatic.

# 29 Elgol

**Length:** Up to 9 miles (14.5km)
**Height climbed:** Undulating; 650ft (200m) on long return route
**Grade:** A/B
**Public conveniences:** Elgol
**Public transport:** Post bus service from Broadford

*A long circuit on rough footpaths and quiet public roads. Some care needed in places, but matchless views of the dramatic Cuillin Hills on clear days.*

To reach the start of this route, drive 14 miles (23km) south of Broadford on the winding B8083, which ends at the little settlement of Elgol on the slopes above Loch Scavaig, near the end of the Strathaird peninsula. As the road drops down towards the shore, look for the car park on the right-hand side.

To start the route, walk back up the road for a short distance, then turn left along a track (initially tarmac) behind some houses, signposted for 'Gàrsbheinn'. By the last of the houses there is a sign for a footpath to Coruisk. Follow this.

The rough path starts along a steep, grassy slope, with wonderful views (even from the earliest sections of the route) across Loch Scavaig to the island of Soay and the craggy peaks of the Cuillins. Beneath Ben Cleat the slope becomes even steeper, and sufferers from vertigo may not wish to follow the path any further. For the rest, continue across the foot of Glen Scaladal (crossing the burn can prove difficult when it is in spate, but it can usually be achieved dryshod), then on along the path beyond beneath Beinn Leacach to the bay at Camasunary, with its grassy hinterland overshadowed by the huge buttresses of Sgurr na Stri and Blà Bheinn.

From this point, the shortest return is by the same route. Alternatively, look for the clear track which winds up the right-hand side of Abhainn nan Leac and over the hills to the east. The track runs for a little under three miles (5km) before joining the B8083, climbing to around 650ft (200m) at its highest point. Turn right along the road (generally quiet) for about three and a half miles (5.5km) to return to Elgol.

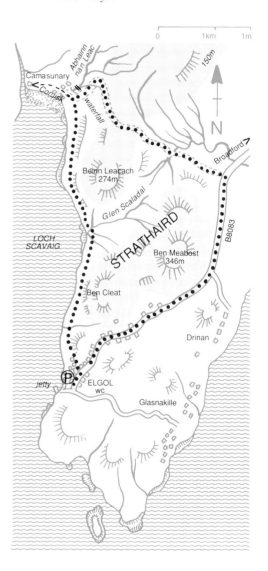

# 30 Point of Sleat

**Length:** 4-5¹/₂ miles (6.5-9km)
**Height climbed:** Undulating
**Grade:** B
**Public conveniences:** None
**Public transport:** None

*A clear, lineal track through hummocky moorland leading to a tiny, rocky harbour, and to the lighthouse beyond. Fine moorland and coastal scenery.*

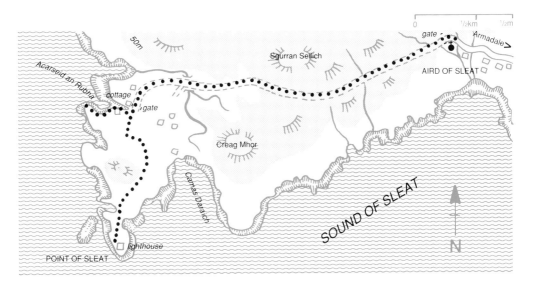

The peninsula of Sleat forms the most southerly part of the island of Skye, with the narrow Sound of Sleat separating it from Knoydart on the mainland to the east. Its scenery is somewhat gentler than that found in most of the island. It boasts, in addition, the pleasant little harbour of Isle Oronsay, and the Museum of the Isles at the Clan Donald Centre, Armadale House (once home to Lord MacDonald: descendant of the old line of MacDonald Lords of the Isles); well worth a visit while you are in the area.

This pleasant lineal walk leads down towards the Point of Sleat. To reach the start, drive south from Broadford on the A851 to Armadale. When the road swings left, down to the ferry pier, carry straight on for about five miles (8km), following the winding single-track road to its conclusion at the small church at Aird of Sleat. Parking is very limited here, and it may be necessary to drive a

short distance back along the road to find somewhere suitable (ie, where you are not blocking the roadside gates and passing places).

Go through the gate at the end of the road and follow the clear track beyond as it meanders through an area of heather moorland, with views over the surrounding sea opening up from the higher sections of the track. Shortly after crossing a bridge over a burn, the track splits. Keep to the right and continue, down to a gate by a cottage. Immediately beyond this, a rough track cuts left, leading a little over half a mile (1km) to the lighthouse on the point.

Alternatively, carry straight on after the gate, down to the tiny natural harbour. A short scramble over the rocks beyond, out to the point to the left of the harbour, provides a fine view southwards to the islands of Eigg and Rum.

Return by the same route.

# 31 Hallaig

**Length:** 5 miles (8 km)
**Height climbed:** Up to 800ft (250m), undulating
**Grade:** A/B
**Public conveniences:** None
**Public transport:** Ferry service to Raasay from Skye

*A fine route on tracks and footpaths of varying quality, passing through areas of woodland, grazing land and moorland, and leading to a deserted township. Excellent views.*

Raasay is a narrow island, running some 15 miles (24km) north to south and lying between Skye and Applecross on the mainland. It is reached from Skye by a ferry running from Sconser – three miles (5km) east of Sligachan – to the pier at East Suisnish. Please note that the distances shown for this route assume the use of a car (though a bicycle would provide more pleasure on these quiet roads) for the four miles (6.5km) to the start of the route.

Turn left from the pier as far as Inverarish, where a road cuts off to the right. Follow this, and at the next junction turn right again and follow the road across the moor to its conclusion at North Fearns. There is space for parking just before the last house on the road, beyond which a clear track continues.

Follow the track along the face of a wooded slope, with fine views across to Applecross and the islands of the Inner Sound. The track soon emerges from the wood and then continues, with the cliffs of Beinn na Leac up to the left, to a turning point above the little headland of Rubha na Leac. At this point there is a memorial cairn to 'the people of Hallaig and other crofting townships' (who were cleared from the land during the last century), and a splendid view opens up of the steep, straight slopes of the eastern coast of the island. Also, in the nearer foreground, there is a fine waterfall where the Hallaig Burn drops over a low cliff into the sea.

Beyond the headland the path gradually deteriorates and finally disappears by the Hallaig Burn. Cross the burn and climb up the slope beyond to visit the deserted township. From this point, either return by the same route or follow the burn up to its watershed and there join the rough path by the side of Beinn na Leac. This path eventually disappears, but not before the public road appears below. Turn left along this to return to the start; right to return to the pier.

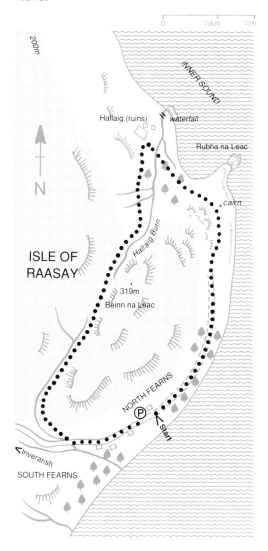

# 32 Loch Oich

**Length:** Up to 8 miles (13km) there and back
**Height climbed:** Negligible
**Grade:** B/C
**Public conveniences:** None
**Public transport:** None

*An excellent lineal walk (with a loop at one end) through an area of broad-leaved woodland by the shore of a freshwater loch. Paths clear.*

Loch Oich is the smallest of the three lochs of the Great Glen, sandwiched between Loch Ness to the north and Loch Lochy to the south. It is some four miles (6.5km) in length and, like its neighbours, forms a link in the Caledonian Canal (between Inverness and Fort William). The straight, steep sides of the glen – a feature of this great fault line along most of its length – are here clothed by woodland. This route runs through the woods along the southern side of the loch.

To reach the start of the route, drive north from Fort William on the A82. Continue on this road through Spean Bridge and on along the side of Loch Lochy. About one and a half miles (2.5km) beyond the end of the loch, just before the road swings to the left to cross the canal, a road cuts off to the right signposted for the lochside walk. Turn up this, keeping to the right when it forks, and park at its conclusion; in the bed of a disused railway with the old platform running along one side.

Walk on along the old railway. After a short distance the track splits, with a smaller path running by the loch side. Follow whichever you prefer (the other can be used for the return). Almost immediately, both these paths cross stiles to enter an area of pleasant, open, broad-leaved woodland comprising the Leitirfearn Reserve. They then continue, in parallel, with views to the left of the loch and its occasional canal traffic.

After a little under one and a half miles (2.5km) there is a further fence, marking the end of the reserve. At this point either return by the path not previously taken or else cross the stile by the lochside path and continue. The further two and a half miles (4km) of clear track leading to Aberchalder are splendid, though it is necessary to return along the same route. Please note that dogs are not allowed along this section.

# 33 Caig Forest Walk

**Length:** 2 miles (3km)
**Height climbed:** 500ft (150m)
**Grade:** C
**Public conveniences:** None
**Public transport:** None

*A pleasant and well-signposted forest walk on clear tracks and footpaths; steep in places, but providing fine views over the surrounding mountain scenery.*

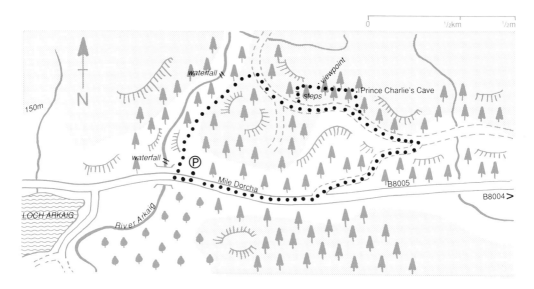

Traditionally, this is Cameron country. Achnacarry, the seat of the Camerons of Lochiel since the mid 17th century (though the current building is of 19th/20th-century construction) lies less than a mile to the south of the start of this route, near the foot of Loch Arkaig. It is also Jacobite country, for Donald Cameron of Lochiel was one of the staunchest supporters of Charles Edward Stuart. Prince Charlie's Cave, on the course of this route, is reputed to have been one of the Prince's hiding places following Culloden.

To reach the start of the route, drive north from Fort William on the A82. At Spean Bridge, continue on the Inverness road. After a mile (1.5km) turn left on the B8004, and at the next junction (immediately after the road crosses the Caledonian Canal) turn right on the B8005 road for Loch Arkaig. Follow this road for around five miles (8km) – at first by Loch Lochy, then turning

westwards – until a car park is reached to the right of the road, just before a large waterfall.

Walk on to the foot of the fall (Loch Arkaig is now visible ahead) and turn right up a clear, steep track through the mature conifers on the slope above the burn. The route has been laid out by Forest Enterprise, and there are signposts along the way to aid navigation.

When the path reaches a forestry track, turn right. After a short distance there is a flight of wooden steps to the left of the track, and a sign for 'Prince Charlie's Cave and Viewpoint'. This steep detour leads to fine views of Loch Lochy, and passes the narrow fold of rocks which may have sheltered the Prince, before rejoining the main track. This then drops down to the public road – the Mile Dorcha (Dark Mile): so-called for its steep, mossy sides and thick tree-cover.

Turn right to return to the start.

# 34 Ben Nevis

**Length:** 10 miles (16km)
**Height climbed:** 2300ft (700m)
**Grade:** A
**Public conveniences:** Fort William, Glen Nevis
**Public transport:** Bus and rail services to Fort William

*A most dramatic route on clear but very rough paths (plus a section along public roads), avoiding the summit, but visiting a vast corrie flanked by imposing cliffs. The use of a good map is recommended.*

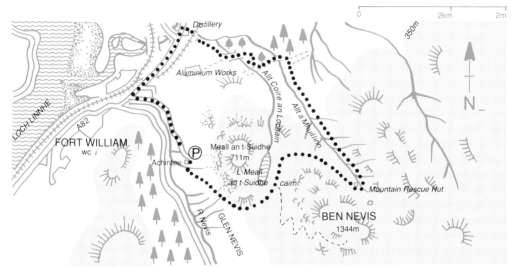

Ben Nevis needs no introduction: the vast rounded bulk of Britain's highest mountain, looming above Fort William, is a familiar image. The route to the summit is gruelling but well-marked, for those who wish to follow it. However, it is also extremely busy – particularly in the summer – and some walkers may prefer something quieter.

Start as for the summit walk. Drive (or walk) north from the town centre on the A82. Almost immediately after crossing the River Nevis turn right up the road signposted for Achintee. Follow this narrow road out of the built-up area and along the lower slopes of Glen Nevis. After a little under one and a half miles (2.5km) the road ends and there is a car park (often busy).

Walk on beyond this along the clear, rough, summit path; climbing steadily and gradually curving round into the col beneath the summit. Above the lochan here the path splits at a cairn.

Turn right at this point to reach the summit – about three miles (5km) distant and a climb of around 2300ft (700m) – or (for this route) turn left instead; along a narrower path which skirts the large buttress to the right and then swings up to the Mountain Rescue Post near the head of Allt a' Mhuillin; surrounded by towering, broken cliffs.

Cross the burn at this point and follow the faint path down the far side. Near the edge of an area of conifer forestry the path joins a clear track. Ignore the track cutting off to the right and continue, across a bridge and on. When a track cuts off to the right, take it; zig-zagging down to the foot of the hill. Once on the flat, the track crosses the Allt Coire an Lochain, shortly beyond which a path cuts off to the right, signposted for the main road. It joins this just beside the distillery.

Turn left and continue for a mile (1.5km) to return to the Achintee road end.

# 35 Achriabhach Forest Walk

**Length:** 2 miles (3km)
**Height climbed:** 500ft (150m)
**Grade:** C
**Public conveniences:** None
**Public transport:** Bus service from Fort William
in summer

*A steep forest walk, largely through mature
conifers, leading to excellent views of the
dramatic mountain scenery of upper Glen
Nevis. Well signposted and paths clear.*

Glen Nevis is one of the most beautiful of Scottish
glens: narrow and winding, with woods and
forestry along much of its length. It curves round
the southern edge of the massive bulk of Ben Nevis
*(34)*, with the elegant peaks of Mamore Forest
rising to the south. A single-track road runs seven
miles (11km) up the glen from Fort William, and
when it reaches its conclusion (at a large car park
by a fine waterfall) a rough track continues; up
onto the wet wastelands around the head of the
Abhainn Rath.

For this route, however, drive just five miles
(8km) up the glen and park in the small car park at
Achriabhach, opposite a house and just before the
road crosses the river. At this point Forest
Enterprise have laid out a route through the
conifers, climbing up to a viewpoint.

Start walking up the forestry track behind the
car park, but take the first turn off to the left
(marked by a post). Follow this rough but clear
path up the edge of the forest, with an open hill of
grass and bracken to the left and the conical peak of
Sgurr a' Mhàim beyond.

When the path joins the main forest track once
more, at a hairpin bend, carry straight on up a
steeper section, with a succession of waterslides
and rapids in the Allt a' Choire Dheirg to the left of
the path. When the burn is in spate (not a rarity,
given the area's rainfall) this can be dramatic.

When the path rejoins the main track once
more, turn left for a short distance; then right, up a
rough path, to reach the viewpoint overlooking the
hills around the upper part of the glen.

Either return by the same route or else follow
the main track down. After the second hairpin a
straight, steep path (marked by a post) drops down
towards the start, providing another possible
variation *(see map)*.

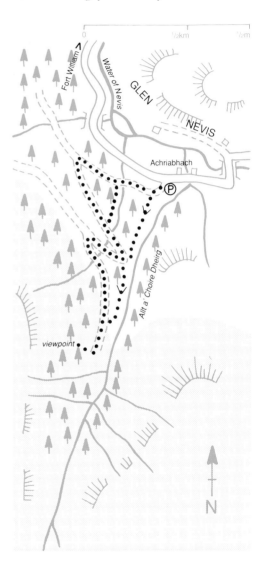